TABERNACLE

PROTECTING THE PRESENCE OF GOD

DIANE EHRLICH

Tabernacle, Protecting the Presence of God
© 2013 Diane Ehrlich

Scriptures taken from the Holy Bible, New International Version ®, NIV®, Copyright © 1973, 1978, 1984, 2011 by Biblica, Inc.™ Used by permission of Zondervan.
All rights reserved worldwide. www.zondervan.com

Scripture quotations taken from the New American Standard Bible ®, Copyright © 1960, 1962, 1963, 1968, 1971, 1972, 1973, 1975, 1977, 1995 by The Lockman Foundation. Used by permission. www.lockman.org

Published by Reform Ministry Publications
Cleveland, Ohio
www.reformministry.com

ISBN 10: 148487207X
ISBN 13: 9781484872079

TABERNACLE

❦

**"Come, let us return to the Lord…
that we may live in his presence." (Hosea 6:1-2)**

CONTENTS

acknowledgements

I want to thank The Holy Spirit for dropping the word "priesthood" into my spirit and asking me to look into it. I knew He was referring to the Levitical priesthood at the time of Moses. At first I hedged and replied, "I really don't want to study the priesthood because it seems too complicated and too boring!"

How wrong I was! The Holy Spirit, my Teacher and Friend, opened my eyes to see the benefits of God's increased presence due to this ministry. The priesthood of all believers is simple, stunning and easy to participate in! I love all that He taught me through this piece and I thank God for His control of my life.

I would also like to thank a few people for their prayers and well-wishes. They are: my prayer partner Diane Office, who prays for me every day, my parents, Melba and Harold Ehrlich, my Pastors Nate and Brisy Ortiz of R.E.D. 4 Christ Ministries, who respect and value the presence of God, and my special friends, Rick and Libia Montalvo, Tami Pepin-Bus and Marilyn Woods. Thank you everyone for your encouragement and support.

FORWARD

The presence of God is the single-most valuable possession of the Church. The engaging power of the Holy Spirit is the sign of God's endorsement of our worship and our message. As we present ourselves to hear God's heart, He speaks and releases us into expressions of Christian service that glorify Him. Without Him, we do nothing of eternal value.

If any Christian fellowship or ministry stops relying on the aid of the Holy Spirit and substitutes methodology instead, it degenerates into a powerless, lifeless form of religion. A vibrant, active relationship with Jesus is what makes the Christian faith distinct from all man-made religions, confirming its validity with Heaven-sent power.

For that key reason, God's presence among us must be honored, respected and protected. This book was written as a reminder to Christians to prioritize Emmanuel—"God With Us" and to keep our first love ministry first. As we learn how to minister to the Lord, we can corporately become the kingdom of priests that God will passionately inhabit.

"Come, let us return to the Lord...that we may live in his presence." (Hosea 6:1-2)

Diane Ehrlich
Reform Ministry, 2013

INTRODUCTION

❦

From Genesis to Revelation we read in the Bible and will present in this book God's express intention to dwell with man by His Spirit. God is for us and He wants to be with us more than we know. One of the ways God shares Himself is by flooding our atmosphere with His presence, touching people who are dulled by the world's adversity and rescuing them with His life. This supernatural phenomena known as "revival" is the refreshing from Heaven that meets our direst of human needs.

Christians who understand the value of God's visitation can learn to welcome His presence individually and corporately. The practice of ministering to the Lord will be explained at length in this book. We will learn why His presence needs to be protected from activities that are repulsive to Him. Our aim is to understand God's pain, His pleasure and His passion as we interact with Him through deliberate relationship. From that insight, we bring Him repentance and worship that endears Him.

As we minister to God, we confidently position ourselves in His love for us and then actively pursue Him. Although He is wondrously vast and unfathomable, He is also immanent, personal and responsive. God is sep-

1

arate from us yet available to us. He is not aloof and out of reach as those who would accuse His character might say. On the contrary, God's involvement with man is most accurately described by the psalmist who tried to comprehend the loving disposition of the Creator towards people. **"When I consider Thy heavens, the work of Thy fingers, the moon and the stars, which Thou hast ordained; what is man, that Thou dost take thought of him? And the son of man, that Thou dost care for him?" (Psalm 8:3-4)**

God longs to be man's exclusive object of worship and possess an adoring holy people for Himself. The cadence, "I will be their God and they will be My people," is unmistakably heard throughout the Old Testament. Ideally, God and man give themselves to each other in undivided, unashamed, naked love.

In the Book of Genesis Chapter 2, we witness the Creator who carefully fashioned man as His crowning masterpiece and placed him in a lush garden where he lived with God under optimum, harmonious conditions. God was pleased with this amazing cohabitation and never wanted it to end. Adam and Eve were clothed in God's splendid light and were indwelt by God's Holy Spirit. They were compatible with God and complete in Him.

By man's own sorrowful choice, this delightful utopia was shattered by rebellion resulting in disobedience. Man willfully divorced his divine Lover by embracing the empty promises of the serpent instead of the commands of God. Darkness, death and dying took the place of light and life as the Spirit departed from them. We will cover this more in Chapter One.

Even so, God pledged to bring man back to an intimate union with Himself with the added dimension of filling man with a fiery hatred of sin and for its perpetrator who is the devil. **"And the Lord God said to the serpent...**

I will put enmity between you and the woman, and between your seed and her seed." (Genesis 3:14-15)

With the invitation to come back into God's presence also came the ultimatum to leave sin behind. This was the command to "repent." Webster's definition of the prefix "re" is "again or back." The word "pent" means "to be held or kept in." The Greek word from the New Testament means "to change one's mind." In the biblical context, repentance is man's informed decision to change his mind to leave his life of sin, turn to God and be closely held anew as in the beginning. God gladly made this restored position possible at Christ's expense because God loves us ever so much. We will look at some things that hinder the restoration process in Chapters Two, Three and Four.

The prophet Isaiah looked ahead and spoke of a Son given to mankind whose name would be "Immanuel" which means "God With Us." The name of God's Son bears the stamp of God's pledge to reconcile man to Himself. This Son is Jesus, whose name carries a slight variation in the New Testament. "Emmanuel" means "to embark upon a vessel, to board ship, to enter or come into." Through this translation, we see God's relentless commitment to restore man to Himself by promising to indwell him again by His Spirit. Through Christ, "God With Us" also becomes "God Within Us" via the indwelling Holy Spirit. God's desire to dwell with man and within man in order to secure and stabilize his affections is God's unalterable plan that will progress from this age into eternity. **"Behold the tabernacle of God is among men, and he shall dwell among them, and they shall be his people, and God Himself shall be among them." (Revelation 21:3)**

Thus the human heart, at one time beating with excitement for sin, is recaptured and redirected back to beating with love for God by the power of the Spirit. Man's supernaturally re-created inner sanctuary becomes the place of meeting for the Holy One and repentant man. The original Garden of Eden experience is restored through Jesus to the utter delight of God. **"Do you not know that you are God's temple and that God's Spirit dwells in you? ...For God's temple is holy, and you are that temple."** (1 Corinthians 3:16-17) The Kingdom of God is accessible within the breast of believers who have invited Jesus to "board their ship" and become their Captain.

God speaks of His union with man in terms of marriage. The marital relationship is the most intimate and fulfilling experience that a man and a woman can have. The couple is so perfectly matched and complimentary that the individual persons become one. Traditionally, newly married couples go on their honeymoon where they are secluded and totally focused upon one another, holding each other breast to breast.

Using marriage as the illustration, "tabernacle" means "habitation, home or dwelling place" where God holds His people close with His invading felt presence. We were created as the object of His love and we respond by gazing into His face through ardent worship of Him. We must see Jesus not only as the Lamb of God who was slain as the atoning sacrifice for our sin, but also as the prescribed way that we may enter the most holy place where God dwells. The indwelling Holy Spirit is our beloved Usher who moves us into God's sacred throne room though worship, prayer and the truth. In Chapters Six, Seven and Eight we will study examples how to minister to the Lord, protect His presence and stand in the gap with right intercession.

The goal of this book is to draw people into worship. Ministering to the Lord is the Church's "first love" ministry. **"You have left your first love...Remember from where you have fallen..." (Revelation 2:4-5)** As you read this material, see it as an invitation to come to the high and holy meeting place in order to tabernacle. We can know the reality of this place in Christ by becoming the surrendered holy people that God enjoys.

God will take us to the place of His presence because we belong there. By the power of the Holy Spirit, we abide in Christ. When we are careful to repent from the offense of sin, we can sustain His prevailing presence. God not only wants to give His people a glimpse of what is in store for them in Heaven, but also offer this wonderful relationship to a world that is dying without Him. Let us enter God's presence by the blood of the Lamb, and see what is necessary to stay and thrive there!

❦

JOINING AND SEPARATING

To appreciate God's relentless commitment to dwell with man by His Spirit, we have to look at what God has been doing since the beginning of time. This chapter will trace His marvelous efforts to join people to Himself, the separated state that we now endure due to sin and the astounding course of redemption that God enacted through Jesus Christ.

Genesis 1:1 is the start of God's discourse with mankind as He communicates to man's intuitive senses. God speaks of His existence through the evidence of the creation as man explores the natural world around him. **"The heavens are telling of the glory of God; and their expanse is declaring the work of his hands. Day to day pours forth speech, and night to night reveals knowledge." (Psalm 19:1-2)**

God entreats man to behold the meticulous design of the heavens and the earth, and come to the conclusion that formative power comes from the Creator. God exhibits His abilities through the created world. Only divine power can create something out of nothing, enabling our planet to function and sustain life. This should be man's reasonable perception. **"O Lord, our Lord, how majestic is Thy name in all the earth,**

**who hast displayed Thy splendor above the heavens!"
(Psalm 8:1)**

God is separate in essence from us in that He is not a created being. He is distinct, unique and exists completely alone in who He is. This is called the "transcendence" of God. No matter where you look, there is no one else like Him. There is nothing or no one that is above Him or more powerful than He is. Nothing or no one can enhance Him or detract from Him. He is complete, perfect and without fault, weakness or defect in any way. His divine Being transcends all creatures and every created thing to the ends of the universe in all realms, seen or unseen. **"For by Him all things were created, both in the heavens and on earth, visible and invisible, whether thrones or dominions or rulers or authorities…"** (Colossians 1:16)

By observing the creation, people can surmise what God is like. He has fashioned a startling variety of plants, animals and physical elements ranging from the immense to the microscopic. The creation illustrates God's orderly, delicately balanced, impeccable design. Therefore, we can say that God has an intelligent plan of harmony, co-existence and inter-dependence. That ideal atmosphere on earth reflects His orderly, peaceful rule in Heaven.

The magnitude of creation also verifies that man does not possess within himself inherent power, ability or knowledge to either create something out of nothing or re-create anything that was destroyed. Man is simply a constituent of the creation. We are here because God placed us here. Although we are able to pro-create (i.e. have babies) we do not have divine power to initiate creation. Created beings, by definition, cannot create themselves nor create anything else. We were made by God's command, not by any initiative of self. We did not will ourselves to be born and, once we entered the earth, we only have the ability to breath, move, think and live. **"...for in Him, we live and move and have our being..." (Acts 17:28)**

Continuing in Genesis 1, to God's glory He took a formless mass and spoke to it, thereby separating things to make them distinct in character, function and purpose. **"And the earth was formless and void, and darkness was over the surface of the deep; and the Spirit of God was moving over the surface of the waters. Then God said, 'Let there be light'; and there was light." (Genesis 1:2-3)** God created the sun and the moon to govern time, and give us a way to measure our days. **"And God made the two great lights, the greater light to govern the day, and the lesser light to govern the night... and to separate the light from the darkness, and God saw it was good." (Genesis 1:16-18)**

The routine of sunrise and sunset of each day quietly speaks to human society, reminding us that we are finite beings, that our lifespan on earth is limited and our days to be alive are numbered. The constant ticking of our biological clock is a subtle reminder that we would do well not to waste our precious time. Our lifespan should be treated as a sacred gift from God and our use of time should compliment His intentions.

The moon, which is the lesser light in the sky, is only bright due to reflected light from the sun. It possesses no light of its own. The relationship between the sun and the moon gives us the example of an object which is dependent upon an outside light source, which is man's condition before God. Without the sun, the earth and other planets of our galaxy would be in utter darkness. The separation of light and dark also serves as a symbol of spiritual light and darkness, which is truth and error. The light of understanding that comes from God allows man to believe in God, understand Him to some degree and be able to distinguish truth from lies.

In all this, God reveals Himself as a rational Supreme Being, exhibiting character qualities of being intellectual, sensible, thoughtful, responsible and educational. God is glorified by His display of power through the creation but He utterly outdid Himself with the inception of man created in His image. Through man, God reveals Himself as a Creator who is relational. He is Someone who we can know. He not only tutors our minds but also nurtures us as living persons. **"Let us make man in Our own image... and God created man in His own image, in the image of God He created him, male and female He created them." (Genesis 1:26-27)** Unlike the rest of creation, we were made specifically for relationship with Him. Let us always keep this in mind.

His relational attributes do not reduce His immensity, but compliment Him as a Loving God. He remains boundless yet tenderly personal. He issues commands that the elements must obey, but He also listens and answers us. Above all, He has delineated Himself as the compassionate Father of the family of those who accept Him by faith and believe in His name. **"For this reason, I bow my knees before the Father, from whom every family in heaven and on earth derives its name..." (Ephesians 3:14-15)** God further extends His relational qualities through human society to include marriage between a man and a woman, children, family members, companionships and societal bonds that enhance the quality of human life.

The whole reason for our existence is to know God through Christ, enjoy relationship with Him, listen and learn from Him, obey His voice and develop ourselves in maturity through the purposes that He has for us. That is what it means to "glorify" God. **"For you have been bought with a price; therefore glorify God in your body." (1 Corinthians 6:20)**

Again using the example of the sun, moon and stars, human lives are meant to revolve around God and reflect the light of His character. Our activities should be directed by Him as we purposely engage Him to seek His will. God always intended for His children to be joined to Him by His Spirit during their earthly life and then remain with Him forever. In eternity we will actually be able to see our Heavenly Father whom we knew by faith on earth. Then we will know the mysteries about Him that we now only know in part.

On the seventh day of creation God performed two specific acts. First, He blessed the day. To bless in Hebrew is "barak" which means "to congratulate, to praise and to celebrate." God was glad that He had made the heavens and the earth, and He was especially satisfied with man as His suitable companion. God looked over His handiwork and called it very good. Therefore, He was deserving of a day of congratulations and praise coming from the creation, acknowledging all that He had done.

Secondly, He sanctified the seventh day. **"Then God blessed the seventh day and sanctified it…" (Genesis 2:3)** The word "sanctified" is the Hebrew word "qadash," which means "to pronounce clean, to declare holy and to keep pure." So God set apart the seventh day, the Sabbath, for man to celebrate and honor the works of God and to keep a holy day that was suitable for His presence. God designated a day, a place and a people with whom to share Himself by His presence on the Sabbath.

Realizing that God is omnipresent or present everywhere, I believe that on the seventh day God flooded the Garden of Eden with His glorious presence as a sign of His pleasure. Everything was bathed in the light and life of God. The earth tasted the vibrancy of Immanuel. The Tree of Life supplied the eternal power for all living things and the Garden of Eden was the holy meeting place for man to worship his God.

At the dawn of time when God blessed and sanctified the seventh day, He had a place on earth that matched His holy dwelling in Heaven. He was able to fill it with His presence because that place was conducive to His holiness. Just as Heaven is centered around God's throne, now the earth had a designated place for worship. The Garden of Eden became God's tabernacle where Adam, His priest, could minister to Him on the Sabbath.

God set one day aside in Adam's week to worship God and tend to His presence. Six days Adam worked as steward of the earth, but on the seventh day Adam tended to his relationship with God through worship. The Garden of Eden became an extension of God's kingdom. **"Heaven is my throne and the earth is my footstool." (Isaiah 66:1)** The seventh day was a day to acknowledge and celebrate God's work in the creation, His greatness and His goodness. It was a time for man to halt his earthly activities and pay attention to Heaven, looking to God who was the source of it all. Caught up in the heavenly romance, Adam declared his love to God and gave Him grateful thanks as the Creator and Sustainer of all life. This ministry of willing worship delighted the Creator.

As a result, everything about this setting was good, enjoyable, interesting, satisfying and right for both God and man. Man had meaningful work on earth and spiritual fulfillment as a priest unto God. Adam and Eve's world revolved around their relationship with God, learning from Him as He spoke to them breast to breast. Adam and Eve also had each other to share their excitement of all they were experiencing in their daily life. This was the heights upon which our original parents dwelt. They had a triangle of unbroken friendship with Immanuel. No secrets were possible because they had utter trust and naked disclosure. At this point, man and woman were innocent. They knew God through pure adoration and they saw themselves as dependent recipients of God's provision. Man came to God for life, guidance and to have his physical needs met. But he also enjoyed God because man knew he was beloved by Him. To His utmost pleasure, God joined Himself to man in the honeymoon experience of worship in the Garden. This was tabernacle at its finest.

SEPARATION COMES

In their innocence, the first human couple never dreamed that their refusal to heed the warning of their divine Lover would cost them their idyllic world. Creational bliss was shattered and destroyed because of their erroneous beliefs and subsequent defiant actions. Through a single event, intimate friends suddenly became mortal enemies. How could this possibly happen?

In the midst of the Garden of Eden, Satan occupied the Tree of Knowledge of Good and Evil. There was actually nothing good about this knowledge. Essentially it was a lower knowledge that the devil carried with him to earth after he was thrown out of Heaven. The devil had a horrible anti-God corruption within him, but also first-hand knowledge of God's goodness from his stay in Heaven. The knowledge of good and evil was a combination of the two that had the potential to produce morality at the person's own discretion, even to the point of twisting things by calling good evil and evil good. The devil's moral corruption was contained in this one place as long as Adam and Eve did not eat the tainted fruit as God commanded them. **"…but from the tree of knowledge of good and evil you shall not eat, for in the day that you eat from it you shall surely die." (Genesis 2:17)**

At the scene of Genesis 3, Satan indwelt a serpent and engaged Eve in conversation. Gradually yet adeptly, he led Eve down the slippery slope of doubt and distrust as he insinuated that she was missing out on a realm that was even more fantastic than what she already knew. Supposedly there was something else for her to experience that was better.

He created dissatisfaction by posing thoughts that she could have the same capabilities as God Himself. The devil's "mind candy" was to promise her god-like personal power. With the idea of having the creation at her command lodged in her head, Eve left the reality of her side-by-side position with God and became lost in the fantasy of replacing Him with herself. The new knowledge would give her unlimited wisdom to become like the Creator rather than live contently under His care. The devil did not tell her that her choice to live independently as her own moral agent would cost her dearly by forfeiting the relationships that she loved the most.

Sound reasoning should have told her that it was not possible to have two Creators. A created being cannot also be Co-Creator because people do not have the power to create anything themselves. What the serpent was suggesting was impossible. But she pictured it in her imagination and her faulty conclusion was, "If I can see it in my mind, then it must be so." On that basis, Eve entered into a huge mystical hoax based on subtle undisclosed lies.

The serpent baited his hook carefully with the promise of power, but the barb that caught and pierced her the most was the accusation that God didn't really love her. This was huge for the woman who was fashioned to be the object of love for both man and God. The thought of being unloved cut her to the very core of her identity, which deeply wounded and confused her. In her emotional turmoil she tragically acted upon the thoughts in her mind. In her heart, she left the relationship with God and reached for the poisoned promise that would make everything she saw "Mine!" The knowledge that she ingested from the fruit lowered her eyes off of God and onto herself, giving her a self-serving perspective. This is the frame of reference that we all suffer from now.

Adam listened and sympathized with his disenchanted wife. He joined her in her fantasy desire to be equal with God by also eating the forbidden fruit. They both gave up their relationship with the Father of their souls in order to have a new-found relationship with the Father of Lies. Sin was introduced to the creation through Adam. Instead of being filled with the Holy Spirit, the place inside of them was now filled with the knowledge self-deification. This was the ultimate divorce betrayal to God. **"Like Adam, they have broken the covenant—they were unfaithful to me there." (Hosea 6:7)** Their failure to obey threw all of creation into a downward tailspin, introducing separation and death, just as God had warned.

We have to pause here to try to comprehend the emotional pain from rejection that this first couple hurled at the heart of God. The purpose of this study is to focus on the heart of God to realize His pleasure, His passion and also His pain. We want to understand how He felt as a cast-off Lover. The re-occurring assault upon God's heart of love from the beginning of time until now creates the need for ministering to the Lord.

In His vulnerability to us, God's heart was pierced by Adam and Eve's betrayal. God stationed an appointed angel with a flaming sword to post guard to forbid any re-entrance to the Garden after the couple's expulsion. The Bible says that the flaming sword **"turned every direction." (Genesis 3:24)** That means that whenever Adam and Eve longingly looked back to their previous home, they would see the fiery judgment sword that severed their intimate union with God. That fearsome sight would remind them, "You pierced Me with your disbelief and denial of what I had told you!" God symbolized His anger, pain and disapproval with the appearance of a fiery sword.

In his book, *From the Cross to Pentecost,* Bishop T.D. Jakes re-tells the infamous scene this way. "The rejected God looked at fallen man and woman, and in his anger that is only known by a rejected lover, He said 'Get out!' We can only get angry when we have loved that much. Out of the depths of pain that Adam's rejection produced in the heart of God, He commanded Adam, 'Get out of the Garden! Take Eve, take your stuff, and get out!' That was what was happening here."[1]

Mankind was never meant to be separated from God, much less joined to supernatural evil via acceptance of the devil's lies. To make matters worse, people were never meant to be emotionally joined to the creation through the false hope of owning everything that they see. Fallen man abandoned his love relationship with God in order to run after his newly found love of self and the worship of the wealth of the earth. Because they reached for the forbidden fruit, people now muster a self-serving energy in hot pursuit of created things with the excitement of making them "Mine!" This mis-spent love is one of the greatest complaints that God vocalizes in the Bible because of the separation that it causes. **"For they exchanged the truth of God for a lie, and worshiped and served the creature rather than the Creator, who is blessed forever. Amen." (Romans 1:25)**

Even so, in His supreme love and mercy, God clothed Adam and Eve with the covering of a sacrificed animal before He sent them away. The blood of an innocent animal was shed to cover the offense of the guilty. The protocol of substitute death, which is the basis of redemption, was established on man's behalf. This exemplifies

---

1   *From the Cross to Pentecost,* P. 42

the passion of God who looked past His own pain, His own offense and swiftly covered that first couple with the means of redemption.

God also preserved and protected the Tree of Life, which was the promise of life eternal for mankind. Man had the hope of dwelling with God forever under the auspices of redemption. This was God's sign that He would make a way for them to come back into His presence because He was committed to living with them as Immanuel. Although God's heart was truly pierced, He still wanted them back. Adam and Eve no longer had the tabernacle experience of the Garden flooded with God's holy presence. Instead, they could come back into God's presence through animal sacrifice to provide a temporary covering or atonement for their sin. As a prototype of the work of Christ, this was now the only way to approach God. There was absolutely no other designated way.

SEPARATION THROUGH MAN-MADE RELIGION

In right response to God's revealed mercy, Adam and Eve taught their sons Cain and Abel to celebrate the Sabbath and come into God's presence through animal sacrifice. **"So it came about in the course of time that Cain brought an offering to the Lord from the fruit of the ground. And Abel on his part also brought of the firstlings of his flock. And the Lord had regard for Abel and his offerings; but for Cain and for his offering He had no regard. So Cain became very angry..." (Genesis 4:3-5)** It is important to understand what happened with these two offerings and how separation from God is perpetuated through man-made religion.

The younger brother Abel obeyed his parents and worshiped in the right way as a true follower of God. The Book of Hebrews cites his faith in looking to God for the promise of redemption to live with God forever. **"By faith Abel offered to God a better sacrifice than Cain, through which he obtained the testimony that he was righteous..."** **(Hebrews 11:4)** What was "the testimony" that Abel received from God showing that his offering was accepted and Cain's was rejected? There is a pattern of at least five instances in the Old Testament where burnt offerings of animals were offered up to God in worship and accepted by Heaven's fire consuming the sacrifice. Examples are found in Leviticus 9:24, Judges 6:21, 1 Kings 18:38, 1 Chronicles 21:26 and 2 Chronicles 7:1. In each instance, the fire of God appeared, engulfed and evaporated the burnt offering as the sign of Heaven's acknowledgment. This thrilling and fearsome sight attested to man's right worship of God. **"Then the fire of the Lord fell, and consumed the burnt offering..."** **(1 Kings 18:38)** In like manner, Abel's offering was consumed by fire as a visible sign and testimony of his acceptable worship.

Cain's offering was not accepted because God ignored it. No fire fell from the sky. Here is why. The fallen nature of self-sufficient pride and self-interest had passed on to the sons from the parents. Indulging the self nature, Cain decided to celebrate the works of his own hands by offering up a sacrifice of grain produced from the earth. This was a man-generated, man-made form of worship. Unfortunately, he was publicly humiliated when his offering remained untouched by Heaven. The two paths of obedience and disobedience now separated the first brothers.

God set some very clear boundaries with Cain by correcting him and reminding him of how to worship God rightly. **"Then the Lord said to Cain, 'Why are you** so angry? And why has your countenance fallen? If you do well, will not your countenance be lifted up? And if you do not do well, sin is crouching at the door; and its desire is for you, but you must master it.'" (Genesis 4:6-7) Cain defiantly refused what God told him to do. Instead of being refreshed from his labor by the power of God, Cain insisted on his own way and was taken over by the power of sin just as God warned. His emotions darkened with anger, his thinking was clouded from resentment and he plummeted quickly to the depths of human depravity by killing his brother as the answer to his own despondency.

God's heart was grieved over Cain's skewed decision to vent his anger. God tried to stop Cain before the murder happened. He tried to reason with him and even gave him hope that, if he changed his mind to do things God's way, then his offering would be accepted as well. But Cain's issue was not the offering. He had fallen in love with the work of his own hands and decided that he should take the credit. He wanted to be congratulated if not celebrated for what he had done. The thinking "I tried" lodged within his mind to legitimize his self-will effort. Cain worked hard, he tried hard, he became enamored with his own effort and the grain offering was a gesture that asserted, "God must accept me because I tried." This is the basis for man-made religion.

The illegal offering focused on what man had done and departed from a celebration of what the Creator had done. Instead of worship directed to God for His super-natural accomplishments, it was diverted and re-directed to man's puny efforts. The grain offering of Cain was incorrect, illicit and unacceptable to the Creator. It did not match the ongoing true worship that occurs in Heaven and was not conducive to God's holy presence. So no matter how hard Cain "tried," his offering was rejected because the object of worship was himself instead of God.

Cain could not enter into the presence of God through illegal worship. He robbed himself of a blessing that would have made life easier for him. Cain refused to allow God to be his Master, so by default, sin became his master. He now had a dark power greater than himself at work in his physical body that made him resent God and hate God's people, just like Satan. This intense discontentment, resentment and hatred is what the Apostle Paul writes about in the Book of Romans, warning people of the deadly grip of sin. **"Therefore do not let sin reign in your mortal body that you should obey its lusts, and do not go on presenting the members of your body to sin as instruments of unrighteousness; but present yourselves to God..." (Romans 6:12-13)**

God's confrontation with Cain is called "conviction of sin." God speaks to human conscience to tell us what we are doing wrong in His sight. God now speaks to man through His Word in the Bible. Without the Word of God as our standard, right and wrong are subject to our own opinions. Instead of living in the light and life of union with God, natural man is distant, living astray and following the ideas and desires of his self-serving heart. The New Testament speaks of this condition: **"...that you walk no longer just as the Gentiles also walk, in the futility of their mind, being darkened in their understanding, excluded from the life of God, because of the ignorance that is in them, because of the hardness of their heart..." (Ephesians 4:17-18)**

Spiritual separation was never God's plan. The only hope for man to be re-joined to God is by repentance and through the acceptable sacrifice to atone for sin. Covered by the atoning blood, fallen man can once again tabernacle with a holy God.

REDEMPTION COMES

Redemption is God's strategic efforts to disprove the satanic lie that denies God's everlasting love for mankind. To redeem something means "to buy it back, to recover or set free by paying a ransom price." The term also means "to restore to oneself by making amends." This is the role of the Savior through whom God demonstrated the most astounding display of selfless love at the Cross of Calvary where He redeemed the human race by the blood of Jesus. The cost of Christ's sinless life paid the ransom price to restore sinful man to Himself. Animal sacrifice was no longer necessary as the temporary means of atonement. This was the joy that filled Christ's heart knowing that His sacrifice completed the Father's means of redemption. **"...for the joy set before Him endured the cross, despising the shame..."** **(Hebrews 12:2)**

The blazing fire of passion burned in Christ's heart for the recovery of mankind as He endured the Cross. Afterwards, the fire of the Holy Spirit physically fell upon believers gathered in the upper room on the Day of Pentecost as a visible testimony of Christ's acceptable sacrifice. **"And suddenly there came from heaven a noise like a violent, rushing wind...and there appeared to them tongues as of fire..."** **(Acts 2:2-3)**

In the books that I write, I vividly describe the intricacies and the atrocities of man's fallen condition. Readers may wonder why I spend so much time on the topic of sin because the approach seems so "negative." But we have to understand that glowing against the dark background of human sinfulness is the dazzling light of God's forgiveness of sin and endless efforts to draw man back to Himself. The contrast of our mistakes sharply illuminates God's willingness to forgive, wash clean and make new. The Apostle Paul expressed this comparison when he wrote, **"...but where sin increased, grace abounded all the more." (Romans 5:20)**

The sin of Adam and Eve and Cain was not contained, but spread throughout human society. Eventually there came a point in time when sin was almost everyone's master. When people indulge their own evil ideas, then sin swells like a pregnancy and eventually gives birth to anarchy. That is exactly what happened as people multiplied over the earth. Some followed in the ways of God but the majority of them followed their own ways, refusing to come into the presence of God just like Cain.

This is the lineage and number of years that transpired until the earth fell into utter chaos. Adam lived 930 years and had a son named Seth. Seth lived 912 years and had a son named Enosh. Enosh lived 815 years and had a son named Kenan. Kenan lived 910 years and had a son named Mahalelel. Mahalelel lived 895 years and had a son named Jared. Jared lived 962 years and had a son named Enoch. Enoch walked with God and was supernaturally received unto God after 365 years. Enoch had a son named Methuselah. Methuselah lived 969 years and had a son named Lamech. Lamech lived 777 years and had a son named Noah.

It is significant that we see the number 777 represented by this man's age because it is the number that expresses the perfection of God. In this case, God showed His perfect mercy and perfect justice through Noah. By the time Noah was born, mankind had collectively rebelled against God, resisted God's presence and produced a horribly violent, godless culture. Corporate sin among men had taken over in such a way that men and women lived in constant wickedness. Earth's population was chaotic, dark, void of God's Word and His presence.

In Genesis 6:3, God announced the withdrawal of His Spirit. **"My Spirit shall not strive with man forever."** **(Genesis 6:3)** The Holy Spirit was moving upon the earth, convicting the world of sin and working to reason with people to no avail. This verse tells us that there is an end to God's patience as He attempts to reach man through conscience.

Here we also get a glimpse of the emotions of God and the pain in His heart due to His observance of the intense evil of man, His one-time suitable companion and priest. **"The Lord saw the wickedness of man was great in the earth, and that every intent of the thoughts of his heart was only evil continually. And the Lord was sorry that He had made man on the earth, and He was grieved in His heart." (Genesis 6:5-6)** People had left Him and now He was getting ready to leave them.

Finally God said, "Enough." That is exactly what Noah's name meant. His name comes from the Hebrew word "nuwach" which means "to settle down, to cease, to quiet and to give rest." Through this translation, we not only see God's decision to cease the tension between His Holy Spirit and the utter defiance of mankind but also give the earth rest from the disunity and bloodshed of its inhabitants. He prepared another place of tabernacle where He could once again peacefully co-exist with man. This place was the ark that Noah built by God's command.

"Noah was a righteous man, blameless in his time; Noah walked with God." (Genesis 6:9) It is a credit to God's mercy and grace that He would bring the necessary power to enable a man to resist sin and live in a pleasing manner before God in the midst of such an evil genera-tion. Noah's obedience had somehow ministered to God, giving him great favor. God's heart was soothed by Noah's denial of self-will activity. God allowed Noah to hear His voice and announced to him His plans to destroy mankind. He revealed His plan to cleanse the earth by flooding its surface. **"Then God said to Noah, 'The end of all flesh has come before Me; for the earth is filled with violence because of them; and behold I am about to destroy them with the earth.'"** (Genesis 6:13)

God gave Noah specific instructions on how to build an ark as a means of escape for his family from the outpouring of God's wrath. With the ark, God created another sanctuary of His design, a holy place to tabernacle with a man who loved and worshiped Him. Once the floodwaters came, God used the buoyancy of the ark as an illustration of lifting man up to his original place next to God, preserving his life now and forever by separating him from sin. By faith and innocent trust, Noah did all that God commanded him to do. In Noah we see a man who willfully chose to return to relationship with God, trusted Him for his life and obeyed what God commanded above human reasoning. This is God's standard for human repentance. God accepted Noah's sacrifice of obedience and his righteousness through faith.

The ark was finished after one hundred years of work with the help of his sons Shem, Ham and Japheth. God shut Noah and his family into the ark and the flood waters covered the earth for 150 days, utterly blotting out all life. After the waters receded and Noah stepped out of the ark, he realized that he and his family were saved. Noah's response was humble grateful worship to God. **"Then Noah built an altar to the Lord...and offered burnt offerings on the altar. And when the Lord smelled the pleasing odor, the Lord said in his heart, 'I will never again curse the ground because of humankind...nor will I ever destroy every living creature as I have done.'"** (Genesis 8:20-21) Amazing as this sounds, here we see an example in scripture where God repents of His wrath. God is actually sorry for venting His anger to bring harsh judgment to destroy mankind. Because of Noah's righteous sacrifice of heartfelt worship and grateful thanks, God's heart and emotions were soothed. He turned from His anger and turned His heart back towards man, restoring him as the object of His divine love.

God's heart was so moved by the restored relationship with man that He made a covenant agreement to never destroy the earth and its inhabitants from a flood ever again. Does this mean that God's heart is not going to be grieved by man's sin and disobedience? No. It means that God's binding oath to show mercy is greater than His righteous anger to show wrath. God set a rainbow in the sky as a reminder of the righteousness of Noah. Now, as God looks down upon the earth, His view is forever filtered through the rainbow. It stands as a constant reminder to God of His covenant agreement that He made with the man who pleased His heart so much. Noah brought soothing pleasure to God's heart through his belief and obedience.

God made an example of Noah for all mankind to see. His name is remembered when we see the threat of rain and then we see the rainbow break through the storm clouds. This is the story of a man who became famous with God and then became famous among men. We also see the graciousness of God who is willing to offer mercy, a rescue from sin and a way of escape from its destructive consequences. Every time it rains on earth, we see the rainbow and are reminded of the obedience of Noah.

The prism of the rainbow around the throne serves as a benchmark of how the obedience of one man saved the whole world. The rainbow begs for mercy on man's behalf and gives man more time to come back to companionship with God. It is an invitation to return to God and is a permanent sign of God's willing desire for tabernacle. That ring of color in the sky also represents the "wedding band" of God's marriage covenant with man. This explains the rainbow that is set before the eyes of God within His temple in Heaven. **"Immediately I was in the Spirit; and behold, a throne was standing in heaven, and One sitting on the throne. And He who was sitting was like a jasper stone and a sardius in appearance; and there was a rainbow around the throne, like an emerald in appearance."** (Revelation 4:2-3)

BIBLICAL FAITH

The faith of Noah is the type of biblical faith that is mentioned in Hebrews Chapter 11. **"By faith, Noah, being warned by God about things not yet seen, in reverence prepared an ark for the salvation of his household, by which he condemned the world, and became an heir of the righteousness which is according to faith."** (Hebrews 11:7) Noah raised his eyes off of himself and re-focused upon the Creator, replacing "I tried" with "I trust." Biblical faith results when our hearts rest, "nuwach," upon God instead of trusting in ourselves. It abdicates personal control in preference to God's choices for us, believing that He loves us and has our best interest at heart. In the midst of a threatening, violent and rebellious society, one man chose to believe and trust what God had told him above the norms of depraved earthly standards. Biblical faith is the belief that God has not only the power but also the integrity to do what He says He will do. We act in faith when we fiercely trust the unseen power of God for our life because of restored relationship with the Person of God. Through our faith, God has the opportunity to prove that He is neither limited nor a liar. He honors our choice to believe in Him and responds with appropriate potency for us.

Biblical faith greatly pleases God and ministers to Him. **"And without faith it is impossible to please God, for he who comes to God must believe that He is, and that He is a rewarder to those who seek Him." (Hebrews 11:6)** This verse cites the attitude that God responds to. By faith, we believe that God is who He says He is in the Bible, that He is good and that He has loving intentions towards us. We fall out of agreement with the satanic lies that accuse God's motives and act upon beliefs found in God's Word instead.

Through these accounts in Genesis, we can see the honored priestly position that man originally held, our subsequent problem due to sin and the gracious steps that God took to reinstate us. We also have the foundation for ministering to the Lord. Next we will look at the two calls that go out upon the earth and the redemption of mankind through the faith of Abraham.

climbers versus followers

I n this chapter we will compare biblical faith that greatly pleases God to the system of the world that urges people to live to please themselves. "Babylon" refers to the collective agreement of people to live for the possessions of culture rather than the pursuit of God. The self-serving perspective that that Adam and Eve introduced continues to entice people to live against God's purposes for them. This activity stems from the rebellion of ancient Babylon where people joined together and refused to obey God collectively. "Babylon" exists now as a prevailing spirit that lures people away from serving God in order to serve their own selfish desires. Unfortunately, this comprises most of the human population and brings tremendous pain to God's heart. If we are going to minister to the emotions of the Lord, then we need to understand the background and seriousness of the widespread worship of created things, otherwise known as idolatry, that so grieves God's Spirit.

We pick up with Noah's family who began to re-populate the earth after the flood. God's will for these families was to move across the land and preserve the faith modeled by their forefather. By doing so, they would cover the earth with the knowledge of God and give honor to the One who gave them a new start. God's desire was for man to worship Him correctly, hear His voice and obey Him so that He could bless the earth with His felt presence.

CLIMBERS

One of the descendants of Noah's son Ham was Nimrod who was a dissenter. The Bible says of him, **"he became a mighty one on the earth." (Genesis 10:8)** This description refers back to the time before the flood when the "mighty men" ruled the earth as violent, deified kings who moved God to bring the judgment of the flood. Nimrod was a warrior and a hunter who founded the city of Nineveh, which later became the capital of Assyria. But this was not to his credit.

Like its founder, the Assyrians were later known for their arrogant pride due to their military might. They were cruel conquerors and oppressors who were famous for their use of destructive force. **"Behold, you have heard what the kings of Assyria have done to all the lands, destroying them completely." (2 Kings 19:11)**

Nimrod's empire began in the city of Babel in the Land of Shinar where he and his followers settled. The citizens of Babel corporately refused the will of God by settling down in the plain country rather than moving across the land where God showed them to go. Instead, they banned together and devised a plan to glorify themselves by building a tower that would somehow reach into the heavens by human means. **"...and they said, 'Come let us build for ourselves a city, and a tower whose top will reach into heaven, and let us make for ourselves a name;**

lest we be scattered abroad over the face of the earth.'" **(Genesis 11:4)** In this endeavor we see the same self-willed false worship that defiled Cain, only on a greater scale. The temple that they fashioned echoed the heart of man-made religion, "I try, therefore I deserve to be accepted for what I do!"

The Tower of Babel was erected as both a fortress and a temple. Sources say that the Babylonian astrologers used this monument to study the stars as people began to worship the starry host through Astrology. "Babel" means "gate of god" and by appearance looked like a meeting place for God and man. This was, of course, a false tabernacle that became a seat for idolatry that was not endorsed by the presence of God.

One Bible commentary states: "The city (Babel) once more becomes a cultural focus of mounting human arrogance. Tower (migdol) could be a fortress, prototype ziggurat or temple-mound."[2] A ziggurat was an ancient Assyrian or Babylonian temple built like a pyramid with step-like stories. Supposedly, men could grow closer to God by reaching different levels. This theme of "climbers" is incorporated into many false religions that people follow as they try to work to reach different levels of spirituality.

To the dismay of the tower builders at Babel, the Lord thwarted their plans and exerted supernatural force to dispel them. **"And the Lord said, 'Look, they are one people, and they have all one language; and this is the beginning of what they with do; nothing they propose to do will be impossible for them.'"** **(Genesis 11:6)** He also performed a creative miracle by inventing different languages to produce a barrier of understanding among them, making it more difficult to collectively rebel. Confusion and

---

2   *Bible Commentary*, P. 91

dispersion from the land was another type of judgment from God. Even after the great flood and the great dispersion of Babel, the Adamic self-will nature was not cleansed from man's heart. Regardless of God's judgments, man declared himself to be his own moral agent, attempting to side-step Almighty God and remain independent from Him.

Throughout the Bible, Babylon symbolizes the enterprises of man and what he builds for himself. This spiritual entity is the "city of man" that is established by people who busy themselves with their own predetermined plans rather than seeking God for His will. They abhor what God requires of them because they think He will ruin what they have in mind for themselves. Like the ancient Babylonians, they want to settle down with the amenities of the world and avoid the commands of the Creator because their lives are so precious to them.

There are two calls that go forth across the earth that every person will answer and embrace. The first and most prevalent is the call of Babylon. This is the invitation to come and serve self with the possessions of the world. There is a mystical drawing power about this invisible city that attracts and entices men's senses. **"...keep on, then, with your magic spells and with your many sorceries..." (Isaiah 47:12)** The ancient lie of owning the creation seizes human hearts with spell-like power and holds them captive to the false hope of calling everything they see "Mine!"

Surrender to this call produces a value system characterized by an edgy addiction to created things. The human heart cries, "I want more!" as people are drawn by an unending desire to feed their yearnings. In the realm of Babylon, commerce is king and money is master. Yet, people are never satisfied. **"Whoever loves money never has enough money; whoever loves wealth is never satisfied**

with its income. This too is meaningless." (Ecclesiastes 5:10-11) Man was never meant to fall in love with stuff and be emotionally joined to created things, catering to his own overpowering desires.

A person's value system is determined by what he or she deems valuable to have. People will process in their minds what seems important and those decisions will lodge at their very core. Inner convictions will become apparent by choices people make and the character traits they develop. This is the origin for the expression "the love of money is the root of all evil." For example, some people think that it is important to have a good work ethic while others decide to get by with doing as little as possible. Some people will realize that personal integrity is a valuable trait to have while others will settle for scheming and cheating as a way of life.

The value system of the world is always a lower, more base set of values because it focuses on the things of earth. The primary motive to become rich and famous is launched by selfish "Me first!" competition. Life is relegated to be a game to win, a stage to perform upon or a race to beat others. There are "winners" and "losers" depending upon the best "climbers" who know how to work the system for themselves. Achievement becomes the main goal because it speaks to the "I try" motives of our fallen nature. The pinnacle of the world's system is to be successful in the eyes of others. Supposedly with the right game plan, a person can be a star and have anything that he wants. The lure of Babylon energizes people to climb to the top for the sake of recognition, no matter what the cost to integrity.

The call of Babylon fills people with dreams of luxury, physical pleasure and illusions of grandeur. The personal visions of wealth, power and prestige can be intoxicating. Jesus told a story in Luke Chapter 15 about a prodigal son who got caught up in a fantasy world of what he thought he could have for himself only to become a slave to the world system. This parable stands as a universal warning for people not to spend the one life they have in search of temporary worldly pleasures that will eventually disappoint them. **"For all the nations have drunk of the wine of the passion of her immorality... and the merchants of the earth have become rich by the wealth of her sensuality."** (Revelation 18:3) Those who succumb to the lure of Babylon pursue the sensuality of this world only to miss the reality of Heaven by choosing the temporal over the eternal.

FOLLOWERS

The second call that goes out over the earth is the call to serve God willingly and enthusiastically. This call requires people to quit their self-seeking and accept the purposes that God has for them. This is truly a higher, more satisfying way to live that God makes possible by the power of the Holy Spirit. **"So faith comes by hearing, and hearing by the word of Christ. But I say, surely they have never heard, have they? Indeed they have: Their voice has gone out into all the earth, and their words to the ends of the world."** (Romans 10:17-18) God want us to choose well and have a life that glorifies Him.

God's plans were not thwarted by the Babylonians. His desire to have a people for Himself and His intention to be Immanuel among them would be carried out. After Noah, God raised up another man who wholeheartedly answered His call. Through the lineage of Noah's son Shem, God found another man who would journey with Him in utmost obedience. To give future generations the example of how to live by faith, God traced the life of his servant Abram in the Old Testament. This man's endearing trust in God compared to Noah's faith in pre-flood times.

Abram was later re-named Abraham, which means "father of a multitude." He lived with his wife Sarai, his father and his nephew Lot in the land of Ur which was occupied by the Chaldeans. The Chaldeans were another godless, warring people who were on par with the Assyrians. The family moved from Ur to Haran and then later settled in Terah. After Abraham's father died, God spoke to him about His plans for him, much like He had spoken to Noah.

Once again, God required a man to separate himself from the godless culture that surrounded him and obey God's voice with innocent, trusting faith. God planned to make His Name known throughout the earth by this follower. Abraham journeyed where God showed him, although he did not know the final destination. Instead, he trusted God to show him each leg of the journey as they went. **"So Abram went forth as the Lord had spoken to him..." (Genesis 12:4)** What was distinct about this journey was that, as God disclosed His will to Abraham at different stages, Abraham built an altar to the Lord to offer sacrifices of thanksgiving. **"...and there he built an altar to the Lord and called upon the name of the Lord." (Genesis 12:8)** We see right worship and obedience soothing the emotions of God and endearing Him to gather a nation of people to Himself. Abraham's faith had the effect of reversing the judgment of dispersion. God promised to establish a people for Himself which eventually became the nation of Israel.

At that time, there was a great famine in the land and God commanded Abraham to take his family to Egypt. As they neared Egypt, Abraham realized that his life was in peril on account of the beauty of his wife, Sarai. He knew that the Egyptians will kill him and steal his wife because she was so beautiful. He asked Sarai to say that she was his sister rather than his wife so that his life would be spared.

The Egyptian Pharaoh heard of her great beauty and sent for Abraham and Sarai. Just as Abraham suspected, Pharaoh took Sarai into his household. God showed His faithfulness by striking Pharaoh and his household with plagues as a sign of judgment. Pharaoh was angry with Abraham for telling him that Sarai was his sister instead of his wife, but released them unharmed.

Abraham journeyed back from Egypt and arrived back at Bethel, which was the same place he had started. This would not be much of an accomplishment for a "climber" because he didn't gain very much ground. But for a "follower," this journey had a huge impact. Abraham was able to experience firsthand the opulence and tremendous power of the Egyptian king Pharaoh. He understood the pinnacle destination of self-serving man from observing Pharaoh's courts. He witnessed the endless accumulation of wealth, servants, political power and military might that "climbers" long to have for themselves.

He also experienced the life-threatening terror of being held captive by a powerful tyrant. Abraham quickly realized that his own wealth, physical appearance and adept human reasoning held no promise to preserve his life. This real-life drama stripped him of any self-sufficiency that he may have had. He had to look to God alone for His mercy and power to rescue him.

There were several life lessons that Abraham carried back to Bethel within his heart. First, he learned that God is able to protect and keep those who are His. He rested in the knowledge of God's safe care. Also, the promises that God gave to Abraham were God's responsibility to fulfill. By simply following God's commands, they would come to pass. Thirdly, he realized that because he had received God's mercy to keep him and his wife alive, he also was responsible to show mercy to others. His calling involved seeking God for mercy on behalf of others as God's intercessor.

God wants to build godly character in His servants, not just reputations for them. He needs them to rightly represent Him to the outside world. God made sure that He put His servant Abraham in touch with his own mortality and inability to do anything by his own strength. Abraham quickly exchanged any lingering thoughts of "I try" for "I trust" after his journey to Egypt. After Abraham learned these lessons, God was then able to reveal to him the great promises that He had in store for him. **"I will bless you, and make your name great, so that you will be a blessing... In you all the families of the earth will be blessed." (Genesis 12:2-3)** Similar to Noah, the faith of Abraham would have worldwide impact even for generations to come.

It is both interesting and amusing that God called Abraham out of the land of the Chaldeans where Astrology was actively being developed and employed. Out of a society of "star gazers" who analyzed the heavenly host to know their destiny, God called his servant Abraham and sent him on an unknown journey. How ironic that through relationship with this man, God would speak to him and say, "Look up at the stars and I will show you your destiny! Your offspring will be as numerous as the stars in the sky. I will make you a great nation and through you all families of the earth will be blessed." With this promise, God clearly scorned the man-made system of divination through Astrology. He made Abraham a true "star gazer" in that, every time he looked up into the heavens, he would be reminded of the incredible promise that God made to him and worship Him for it. Because the Chaldeans chose to corporately resist God and used a system to bypass Him in order to know their fate, they utterly missed the true destiny that God had for them.

People miss or ignore the call of God because serving the Lord may seem unattractive, unexciting or too self-sacrificial. "Climbers" who serve the world in hopes of temporal gain have settled for a lesser glory. The gain of the kingdom does not appeal to them because they hold the fantasy of fame and fortune as the only glory to be had. They are blinded by delusions and do not see the truly glorious aspect of the kingdom of God.

M.R. DeHann, M.D. in his wonderful study *The Tabernacle* says, "The outsider, on the outside of the tabernacle, saw nothing of its exquisite beauty. All he was able to see was the drab leather covering of badger skins unattractive, somber and unappealing to the natural eye."[3] The appeal of the kingdom of God does not attract people because it is a call to come and die to self in order to live for the desires of God instead. In fact, it is offensive because the promise of Babylon seems to hold so much more. Until a person becomes disenchanted with the cheap glory of the world and turns away to answer the call of God, he cannot see the splendor of the kingdom. **"Jesus answered and said to him, 'Truly, truly, I say to you, unless one is born again, he cannot see the kingdom of God.'" (John 3:3)** We must be able to "see" the kingdom in order to understand the higher value system that it holds. Actually, serving God is the only pursuit that makes sense once we consider that the world is temporary and the kingdom is forever.

Once a person "sees" the kingdom, his value system should shift to hold sacred the things that are eternal. The most important possession that a person can have is a restored relationship with God through Jesus Christ and

3   *The Tabernacle*, P. 49

the constant sense of God's presence. To know Immanuel is the greatest source of comfort, peace and eternal success that is possible. All of the other benefits of knowing Christ are ours once we have the "pearl of great price" in our life.

Knowing God allows us to know His heart and understand His ideals. We realize that God deems human life valuable, and He is on a mission to preserve human life now and forever. We can know His overall purposes, understand His desire to extend His kingdom and feel the urgency to offer the salvation that Christ avails to every human being. **"Therefore be careful how you walk, not as unwise men, but as wise, making the most of your time, because the days are evil. So then do not be foolish, but understand what the will of the Lord is."** (Ephesians 5:15-17)

Unlike "climbers" who have their lives all planned out for themselves, "followers" realize that God has greater plans for them. They decide not to settle for the glory of man's kingdom but instead believe that God has something that is higher and more glorious. **"But, beloved, we are convinced of better things concerning you..."** (Hebrews 6:9)

Because we have relationship with God through Christ, God will communicate His specific will for us so that we will do the high and heavenly works that He has planned. This puts us on a faith journey seeking God to show us the next step just like Father Abraham. We must be in Christ to know the Father's will for us. Otherwise, we are just doing religious works and expecting God to bless us because "we try." **"For we are His workmanship, created in Christ Jesus for good works, which God prepared beforehand, that we should walk in them."** (Ephesians 2:10)

The faith journey that we embark upon is different from the goal of the world that says, "Achieve."

As "followers" we are required to simply believe and do what God is showing us to do. **"Then they said to him, 'What must we do to perform the works of God?' Jesus answered them, 'This is the work of God that you believe in him who he has sent.'" (John 6:28-29)** Jesus didn't say "achieve," He said "believe." The works of God do not supersede relationship with Him. In fact, the works of God depend upon and flow from our communication with Him at all times. Whatever God shows us to do, it is all for His glory, that His Name would become famous on the earth. He does not expect us to be famous; He expects us to be faithful. **"I bow down toward your holy temple and give thanks to your name...for you have exalted your name and your word above everything." (Psalm 138:2)**

The works of God are God-sized and cannot possibly be done with our natural abilities. They are designed to display God's power, His love, mercy and kindness. They also strip us of self-centeredness, self-reliance and self-righteousness. We discover the power of Christ for us as we travel to where He is showing us to go. **"Bless be the Lord for he has heard the sound of my pleadings. The Lord is my strength and my shield; in him my heart trusts; so I am helped, and my heart exults and with my song I give thanks to Him." (Psalm 28:6-7)**

Whoever follows Jesus adheres to His Word in the Holy Bible and has relationship with Him through the Holy Spirit. We need to be diligent with both avenues of guidance. The Bible transforms our mind and the Holy Spirit transforms our heart. **"Again Jesus spoke to them saying, 'I am the Light of the World. Whoever follows Me will never walk in darkness but will have the light of life.'" (John 8:12)**

We are given very specific instructions in the Book of Galatians to follow God by His Spirit. As followers of Jesus, we do not follow rules about Jesus, but we follow Jesus as He rules. The phrase that the Bible gives is to "walk by the Spirit," which means to live according to what Jesus is currently saying in our relationship with Him. Jesus has very specific places for us to go, things for us to do and people to meet. We must be diligent to make all the appointments that He has for us. He gives us new and interesting things to do that stretch us as individuals and makes us grow up. We accept new responsibilities and shine for Him as capable people. **"But I say, walk by the spirit, and you will not carry out the desires of the flesh." (Galatians 5:16)**

There are benefits to our love relationship with God that the Bible describes in detail. The Book of Deuteronomy clearly says that when we are diligent to love God, obey Him and fear Him, then He will ensure our good health, protection, peace and prosperity. The benefits of knowing God cannot be separated from His presence. It is a biblical "package deal" in order to encourage us in our faith. **"For you are a holy people to the Lord your God; the Lord your God has chosen you to be a people for His own possession out of all the peoples who are on the face of the earth...And He will love you and bless you and multiply you; He will also bless the fruit of your womb and the fruit of your ground...You shall be blessed above all peoples...And the Lord will remove from you all sickness; you shall not be afraid of them; you shall well remember what the Lord your God did to Pharaoh and to all Egypt." (Deuteronomy 7:6, 13-15, 18)**

Because the benefits are so great, it is important to become the holy people that God enjoys having fellowship with. To further exhort us to live by Heaven's standards and in light of eternity, the Apostle Paul tried to describe the rewards that exist for believers as an incentive not to settle for the temporary glory of this world. **"Things which eye has not seen and ear has not heard, and which have** not entered the heart of man, all that God has prepared for those who love Him." (1 Corinthians 2:9)

The glorious wonders of the riches of Christ are only revealed to His followers. Those who dare to set their course to re-claim innocence and live in restored relationship with God will have the thrill of intimacy. Just like the first Adam, they will know the mind, will and emotions of God as, breast to breast, they tabernacle together.

INTERCESSION

Once again, the people of the earth had rejected God and now the sin of the cities of Sodom and Gomorrah was so great that they demanded judgment. Here we see the inter-relationship between God and man as God chooses to confide in Abraham, who is destined to be one of the great kings of the earth. **"And the Lord said, 'Shall I hide from Abraham what I am about to do, since Abraham will surely become a great and mighty nation, and in him all the nations of the earth will be blessed?'" (Genesis 18:17-18)**

As God confides in Abraham about the judgment He was going to bring, Abraham considers the character qualities of God and appealed to Him for mercy instead of judgment. The Bible says, **"While Abraham was still standing before the Lord." (Genesis 18:22)** To "stand before the Lord" is to assume the role of priest, ministering unto God because of a right relationship with Him. It is a position that is obtained through obedience. In this place, God gave Abraham the privilege to respond by asking for mercy rather than immediate judgment. Abraham asked for God to spare the city for the sake of the righteous, even if there were only ten righteous. God was pleased with Abraham's intervention and agreed to those terms.

God weighed the close relationship, right worship, righteousness and obedience of one man against due judgment when Abraham stepped before Him. His anger was temporarily diverted, and God gave Sodom and Gomorrah another chance to repent. From this event, we see our place as Abraham's children to also intercede.

On the basis of this foundation, every spiritual child of Abraham, every believer and follower of God, has the same charge, right and privilege to stand before God to appeal for mercy for others. This is a very biblical way to pray. We are told, **"Listen to me, you who pursue righteousness, who seek the Lord: Look to the rock from which you were hewn, and to the quarry from which you were dug. Look to Abraham you father..." (Isaiah 51:1-2)**

If we were "climbers," we wouldn't care what happens to others because we would be focused on ourselves. But if we journey in obedience as God's "followers," we become interested in the same things that He is interested in and avail ourselves to serve His purposes.

In this age of grace when God holds out the salvation won by Christ to mankind, God expects His followers to join Him in His passion for redemption. Redemption is the global plan set by God to bring His glorious forgiveness of sin to the utter ends of the earth. **"I will make you a light for the Gentiles that you may bring my salvation to the ends of the earth." (Isaiah 49:6)** This is God's heart—to bring the good news of Jesus Christ to all peoples.

All Christian service can be summed up with this underlying cause. God's activity now on the earth is redemptive. This involves the tedious work of winning men's hearts to the message of Christ and bringing people back to right relationship with God. Having a clear understanding of God's passion and purpose for redemption on a global scale moves us to ask the question, "But how can this be done?"

The answer is intercession. Only through the conviction power of the Holy Spirit will men and women awaken to their most basic problem of sin and their need of a Savior. When the power and presence of God breaks through to people's conscience, their awareness of God is heightened. This highlights the need of ministering to the Lord in order to protect His saving presence. Intercessors, such as Noah and Abraham, can be raised up to pray for mercy that will reach people on a grand scale. We have to see the weighty significance of ministering to the Lord in order to give ourselves to it.

Before we do that, let's first look at some of the hindrances that get in the way of answering God's call.

CHAPTER THREE

❦

RELIGION VERSUS RELATIONSHIP

We can see from the lives of Noah and Abraham that God relentlessly works to make Himself known in order to have relationship with people. He continues to use human vessels to bless people with His presence. As we established in the first chapter, God is extremely relational. He wants to be involved with every aspect of our lives. He is not "God out there somewhere." We do not have to guess or make up things about Him because He has revealed Himself through the historical Jesus of the Bible. When we come to know Jesus, we can have daily relationship and communication with Him. We can know the truth about God and it will ring like a bell within us. This is essential for tabernacle.

We also learned in the first chapter that man-made religion, or the celebration of the works of man, is not accepted by God and stands as a barrier to relationship with Him. Since the beginning, man has had the tendency to redefine the nature and ways of God to suit him. Religious activities that people engage in that do not comply with what God actually requires are futile and useless. People participate because these activities trick conscience into thinking that these ways please God. For example, some people give up eating certain foods during the Lenten season before Easter. Yet the Bible does not require that type of self-denial. Therefore, it is important to see how forms of religion keep people separated from God and do nothing to minister to Him. This chapter will cite some well known practices and then examine them for their biblical integrity.

A critical aspect of biblical faith is in believing the right things about God as He has described Himself in scripture. For the purpose of this study, we must emphasize the tie between right doctrine and right worship. Jesus linked worship and truth together in His conversation with the Samaritan woman at the well. **"You worship that which you do not know; we worship that which we know, for salvation is from the Jews. But an hour is coming, and now is, when the true worshipers shall worship the Father in spirit and truth; for such people the Father seeks to be His worshipers. God is Spirit, and those who worship Him must worship in spirit and truth." (John 4:22-24)**

In this passage, Jesus corrected the inquiring woman on her thoughts about the proper location and directed her to Himself as the object of worship. Jesus mentioned the Law that originated with the Jews because it rightly described and pointed to Jesus, who was Himself the fulfillment of the Law. The Samaritan woman no longer had an off-limits place, but a living Person to worship. Relationship with God is founded upon truth. Right doctrine is what keeps us on track for acceptable worship of an unseen God who is Spirit.

The knowledge of Him found in scripture should thrill our hearts and move us into ardent worship. The more we know about Him, the more we stand in awe! People who base their faith on what the Bible says are the worshipers that the Father is looking for because they minister to Him out of their right understanding of Him.

This is important because there are many unfounded notions about God these days that actually fall into the category of superstition. People may repeat certain expressions to frame their world and expect God to endorse these erroneous beliefs. These are simply myths of our culture that have no true spiritual value. Idioms such as "Everything happens for a reason," "What goes around come around," "There is good and bad in everyone. You just have to look for the good" and "I have my own way of understanding God" all seem to express a collection of beliefs. But are those beliefs true? Are people allowed to make up what they want to believe and expect God to honor it with His acceptance? The answer is a resounding, "No!"

An expression that has become extremely popular lately is the statement: "There is only one God but many paths to Him. People can choose their own path no matter what religion they are in." The term for this claim is called "universalism." This holds all religions equally valid in that they all lead people to God no matter what methods they use.

People often passionately defend this all-inclusive faith that ultimately leads everyone to the same God because it seems very altruistic on the surface. It paints a picture of a God who is all-loving, all-embracing and who does require specific doctrine. Those who believe this make themselves seem like good hearted, open-minded, accepting types of people. In their benevolence they say, "If God loves everyone, then why shouldn't He let everyone into His presence no matter what 'door' they choose to come through?" This seems like a rational argument that defends the loving nature of God until we hear Jesus' teaching on whether this statement is actually true.

Jesus explained to the crowds how to enter the kingdom of Heaven. He told His followers what they must do to be accepted into God's presence for eternity. **"Not everyone who says to Me, 'Lord, Lord' will enter the kingdom of heaven; but he who does the will of my Father who is in heaven. Many will say to Me on that day, 'Lord, Lord, did we not prophesy in Your name, and in Your name cast out demons, and in Your name perform many miracles?' And then I will declare to them, 'I never knew you; Depart from Me you who practice lawlessness.'"** (Matthew 7:21-23)

Even though popular ideas in today's culture assure people that they can believe whatever they want because God does not exclude anyone, according to this statement God will not accept them because He never knew them. Entrance into the eternal presence of God is based upon relationship with Him and doing the will of God because of a right knowledge of who He is. Jesus will turn people away from going to Heaven because they made up their own rules about God, which is actually the practice of lawlessness.

Jesus said that He will turn to them and say, "I never knew you." The word "knew" in the Greek is "ginosko" which means "to allow, to be aware of, to perceive, to be sure of, to understand and to speak to." This is in the context of meeting, knowing and understanding someone through a relationship encounter with him.

Jesus stated that He will not accept people who do miracles, prophesies and exorcisms outside of a relationship with Him. Let me clarify that Jesus was not discounting miracles done in His power. Those were the very acts that He sent the seventy disciples out to do in Luke Chapter 10. **"And the seventy returned with joy, saying, 'Lord, even the demons are subject to us in Your name.'"** (Luke 10:17) Jesus was pleased with their results but made sure that their primary goal was to have a seat reserved in Heaven.

**"...but rejoice that your names are recorded in Heaven."
(Luke 10:20)**

Spiritual activities are not the basis for entrance into
the kingdom, no matter how sincere. Heaven is accessed
through relationship, not through religious methods.
Jesus essentially denied the idea of universalism by saying, "I turned you away because you never understood
who I was. You never met Me. You never had a real, via-
ble encounter with Me. You never perceived Me as God,
you were never sure of Me and you never trusted in Me.
Moreover, you never allowed Me to speak to you and you
never accomplished my will. Because you resisted knowing Me on earth, so I resist you in Heaven. Depart from
Me, you who do false miracles rather than My will, I never
knew you!"

We must choose to meet God during this life, turn our
affections towards Him and engage in relationship with
Him. As a result of the impact of this realization, a person
should adjust his life around Jesus because of who He is.
As we get to know Him more and more, we will receive
directives from Him as He shows us what He wants us to
do. We respond by doing what He asks because of our rec-
tified understanding of Him. The fear of God is the mental adjustment we have when God becomes "big" to us and
we appropriately become "small." All of our good works
are done as a result of conversion by Him and then conversation with Him. Good works are not what we "bring to
the table," but what are "on the table" when we come to
"dine" with Him.

To verify this, we see the same meaning of the word
that Jesus used when He spoke of His relationship with
the Father. Referring to the God of Abraham in a discussion with the Jews, Jesus said **"...but I do know Him, and
keep His word." (John 8:55)** Jesus was emphatic that He
had a first-hand experience with the Father and offered

people an accurate account of Him. As a result of rightly knowing the Father, He did the Father's will and kept His Word. Man's entrance into Heaven will carry the same stipulation that Jesus Himself had. Therefore, we must agree to God's terms of the relationship by doing what He asks us to do. There is no other entrance way into the presence of God except through the "door" of His Son. God's welcome depends upon an "I trust" relationship, not an "I try" religion.

THE SHACK

Movements have emerged in our culture with rhetoric fashioned in spiritual terms to somehow help God's non-all-inclusive reputation by "re-inventing" Jesus to make Him more relevant and acceptable to our pluralistic tastes. Unfortunately, this is very shaky spiritual ground.

One of the most disturbing evidences of this phenomenon is presented in the New York Times best seller *The Shack* by William Paul Young. Reportedly over 5 million copies of this theological novel have been sold. Just because something is widespread doesn't make it right or profitable. We live in a day of much knowledge where we are inundated with people's notions and opinions. Biblical faith that is approved by God is belief in the right descriptions about Him that He has given in the Bible. We dare not try to manipulate and bend such statements as: **"For I am God, and not man—the Holy One among you." (Hosea 11:9)** or the First Commandment **"You shall have no other gods before Me. You shall not make for yourself an idol, or any likeness of what is in heaven above…" (Exodus 20:3-4)** in order to make the triune God supposedly more understandable and approachable. The God of the Bible is actually not approachable because

He dwells in a pure, blinding light so that man cannot see Him. **"Who alone possesses immortality and dwells in unapproachable light; whom no man has seen or can see."** **(1 Timothy 6:16)** Jesus came as God's ambassador to represent the unseen Father to us.

Here are some quotes that substantiate the current trend to "re-invent" the Christian faith, including the portrayal of its central figure, Jesus Christ. "Emergent leaders say that the Christian faith needs to be re-invented or re-imagined for the 21st century."[4]

"Many Christians—whether through ignorance or as a result of being poorly trained downplay the holiness of God. God's name is maligned and blasphemed in the culture around us, and it seems that Christians have increasingly absorbed the world's understanding of a God who is fun, who exists for our benefit and who can be the butt of endless jokes."[5]

On the back cover of *The Shack* itself, we read the following statement. "In a world where religion seems to grow increasingly irrelevant, *The Shack* wrestles with the timeless question: Where is God in a world filled with unspeakable pain?"

Ironically, a theologian's take on *The Shack* approves of the author's license for re-invention of deity. "The Shack was distinctive for forcing the reader to confront a truly unthinkable crime…This profound and daring treatment of evil was complimented by a depiction of God that was striking in its innovation and theological sophistication."[6] This same author goes on to say, "But then theologians face the challenge of making the Trinity relevant again."[7]

---

4   *Faith Undone*, P. 16
5   *The Discipline of Spiritual Discernment*, P.P. 49-50
6   *Finding God in The Shack*, P. 2
7   Ibid. P. 9

In striving for "relevancy," the author of *The Shack* has veered off into some key errors such as devaluation of the Word of God, expressed disappointment with God by blaming Him for the course of human evil and then attempting to help God's reputation by falsely representing Him to readers.

Compare the author's derogatory comment about the Bible versus what scripture says about itself. "In seminary he had been taught that God had completely stopped any overt communication with moderns, preferring to have them only listen to and follow sacred Scripture, properly interpreted of course. God's voice had been reduced to paper, and even paper had to be moderated and deciphered by the proper authorities and intellectuals."[8] With similar querulous and caustic dialogue, he beckons readers out of their preconceived notions including sound doctrine.

The Bible does not yield to such sentiment at all. **"All scripture is inspired by God and profitable for teaching, for reproof, for correction, for training in righteousness..." (2 Timothy 3:16)** The Holy Spirit speaks to human hearts through God-breathed passages in the Bible to keep people on track in their relationship to God. Scripture is a sharp, living "sword" that discerns our hearts and directs us into discussion with God about our innermost musings. This is the right combination of Spirit and truth.

Having said this, we have the right light under which to examine *The Shack* to see how the author tries to pad the frightening, holy nature of God with pounds of human flesh and culturally acceptable lingo. The main character Mack is described as having an encounter with "god" in an abandoned shack and is surprised to find his "religious stereotypes"[9] shaken when he meets a large

---

8   *The Shack*, P. 67
9   Ibid, P. 95

Black woman named "Papa" who says she is "god." She is busy cooking up some grub in the kitchen while wearing earphones and listening to some "Eurasian funk and blues with a message and a great beat."[10] Young introduces Jesus as some sort of amicable lumberjack and the Holy Spirit as a translucent female willow-the-wisp who fades in and out. The Lady Wisdom of Proverbs is portrayed as an exacting judge who shakes Mack up enough to bring him to his senses. As a result of his final encounter with her, he stops blaming God for his misfortune and supposedly resolves his inner conflicts. The flimsy caricatures that the author portrays are utterly contemptuous of the personhood of God as the Holy Trinity is tragically defamed.

Undaunted, Young launches into a well-crafted, fast-paced and emotionally charged murder mystery that is liberally sprinkled with statements of an all-inclusive faith and sarcastic jabs alluding to the powerlessness of the Church. The main character complains that he is "sick of all the little religious social clubs that didn't seem to make any real difference or effect any real changes."[11] Such statements do much to color his biases and undermine the mission of the Church.

Supposedly, Mack finds the answers that he needs to give him emotional release from a "great sadness" and the ability to forgive his daughter's killer after his dialogue with the "god" he meets in the shack. "All the changes in his life, he tells me, are enough evidence for him. The Great Sadness is gone and he experiences most days with a profound sense of joy."[12] The book claims to offer "a magnificent glimpse into the nature of God that is not

---

10 *The Shack*, P. 92
11 Ibid, P. 68
12 Ibid, P. 249

often presented in our culture."[13] Overall, we are offered a "new and improved" version of the changeless God of the universe.

Unfortunately, the conclusions that are drawn from *The Shack* are purely conjecture because the real God of the Bible, the historical Jesus and the re-creative Holy Spirit are not offered to readers. We are left with the impression that we can meet with no-gods of our own making to be healed of our brokenness, unforgiveness and pain. We are given written permission to self-medicate with our own versions of Deity that will not offend us. *The Shack* poses God to be on our level rather than someone who is infinitely beyond our understanding. But God's transcendence is the very thing that rescues our heart's cry in that He is able to reach down and take hold of us like no one else can.

God's ministry to the human psyche that brings hope, peace and change is in the revelation of who Christ is, not what we want Him to be. **"And He came and preached peace to you who were far away, and peace to those who were near; for through Him we both have access in one Spirit to the Father." (Ephesians 2:17-18)** The Holy Trinity is available to man through the saving work of the Son, by the power of the Holy Spirit ushering us into the presence of the Father. This is where we can tabernacle with Him to find resolution and peace. Like good medicine, we need the Spirit's revelation instead of man's fast-paced rhetoric.

Let's look at a biblical encounter with the historical Jesus to see for ourselves the miraculous release from a life of great sadness. The life-saving freedom that Jesus actually produces cancels out the need to re-imagine and re-invent Christ. Going back to the Samaritan woman at the well, in

---

13 *The Shack*, P. 254

her attempt to keep the discussion on the surface through religious postulation, Christ broke through and revealed her heart. This is something that only God can do because He sees right through us. Sheer truth is a scalpel that carves away religious pretense that keeps us distant from God.

Let's see her reaction to her meeting with the historical Jesus. **"Come, see a man who told me all the things that I have done; this is not the Christ, is it?" (John 4:29)** In other words, she asked her friends, "Is this no one else but the Christ?" After religion was removed from her, she saw Jesus as Messiah and was set free from the drudgery of her sinful lifestyle. She had a meaningful, intimate experience with the insightful Jesus who knew her better than she knew herself. Now she was released to be His worshiper because she submitted to the truth of who He was.

There was no hype during this strategic encounter. Jesus did not make Himself into a funny clown in order to get her attention. No doubt that this woman was terribly wounded after being served a certificate of divorce by five different men. Who knows the emotional or physical abuse that she suffered because they were not pleased with her? Her rejection sent her running into someone else's arms many times. Yet with careful regard for her monumental pain, Jesus still directed her to see her own sin, her own error and everything that she had done to wreak havoc upon herself. He settled issues with her and then miraculously released her from all guilt and pain. She went running back into town shouting, "What a Savior!" as grace and truth were both dispensed in her life!

The word "relevant" means "to bear upon or relate to the matter at hand." It means cutting through the unnecessary details and getting to the point. Dealing with the current issue that needs the most attention is the way to stay relevant. In this instance and all accounts of the historical Jesus, He was known for getting to the heart of the matter because that is what truth does. He broke through to many veiled hearts as Lord and Savior. Therefore, the historical, risen Christ was and always will be extremely relevant.

Just like the monument built by the people of Babel, *The Shack* is a false tabernacle and a meeting place of man's invention. William Paul Young has not helped people by creating false images and encouraging people to join him in his preferable theology. In his book *Burning Down The Shack*, James B. DeYoung, who was a colleague of William Paul Young, gives this important advice. "The best procedure is to stay as close as possible to the boundaries of the Bible to avoid unforeseen consequences of trying to make God relevant or contemporary."[14] We don't ever want to mislead people in their beliefs about God that, at the end of their life they would be faced by the real Jesus only to hear Him say, "Depart from Me you evil-doers. I never knew you."

ASTROLOGY

The question arises when citing this passage in Matthew 7:21-23, "How are these people able to prophesy, do miracles and cast out demons in Jesus' name without knowing Him and having His power?" This is where the altruistic notion of "one God but many paths to Him" comes into play. People may know about Jesus because His name is famous and powerful. The devil also knows about Him and can mimic some of His miracles with occultic power. With the "new spirituality" that is on the scene that brings people into a "Christ consciousness," it will be very common for people to do things "in Jesus' name" under

---

14 *Burning Down The Shack*, P. 21

the influence of demonic power as they combine various religious teaching, rituals and incantations to produce a form of spirituality. It will be easy for deceived participants acting under the influence of demonic powers to think they are acting on behalf of God because they have not defined their experiences by the Bible.

Let me give some modern examples of different spiritual practices that could result in false prophesy, miracles and dealings with demons. The first practice is Astrology and is used by people to supposedly learn their fate in life by studying the formations of the planets and the stars. As mentioned earlier, the Tower of Babel was employed as both an altar and a fortress, built as a "stairway to the stars." There, the ancients studied the constellations to somehow apply mathematic formulas and arrive at predictions about the future. One author on Astrology verifies this origin in her writing. "The word astrology comes from astro and logos, literally meaning the 'language of the stars.' The earliest known astrological records were found in the City of Babylon in Mesopotamia in the Tigris-Euphrates Valley (present day Iraq.) The ancient Chaldean priests...their observations backed by precise calculations, developed into the science and art known today as Astrology."[15]   The Chaldeans observed the relationships between the planets at the time of a person's birth and they surmised that person's future. This became a form of divination as people sought the starry host for guidance.

Astrologers today claim that people, places and experiences fall under the "ruler ship" of specific planets depending upon their place in the heavens, which is the zodiac. "The zodiac is a division by twelve of the earth's yearly revolution around the sun. Your birthday

15 *Astrology For Enlightenment*, P. 4

determines your sun sign...Each planet 'rules' a specific sign, meaning that the planet 'feels at home' in that
sign."[16]

Astrology is used to give people information about life,
love and vocations. People read their horoscopes according to their birth signs to glean advice and predict what is
in store for them. "A horoscope is a map of the position of
the planets in the heavens at the exact time and place of
your birth. This map represents a circle of 360 degrees...
Astrologers divide this path into 30 degree sectors. These
are the twelve 'signs of the Zodiac' or 'Sun signs.'"[17] Using
these seemingly proven sun signs, converts to Astrology
can map out their life to have a glimpse of their future.
People seek out astrologers to help them chart their
course. "At one point, you may want to have a professional
astrologer establish your personal chart based on your
personal date...This will give you the blueprint of your
life and it will enable you to understand yourself better. It
will also help you plan your life more consciously"[18]

One book on Astrology for beginners asks these questions for the novice to consider as he uses the information
that the stars supposedly give. "How can I bring about a
positive change in my own life?" "What can I, as an individual, do to promote greater harmony in my family, community or my corner of the world?" Unfortunately, this
exploration of divination is often masked by good human-
itarian goals.

Here is why this practice is forbidden by God. The
individual use of Astrology totally bypasses a relationship
with the Creator of the heavenly host to inquire what He
has in mind, therefore it promotes separation from God.

---

16 *Astrology For Enlightenment*, P. 9
17 *The Astrologers Handbook*, P. 3
18 *Astrology For Enlightenment*, P. 36

Astrology has people learning the so-called rules that govern the universe without facing the Governor of the universe. For that reason, the Bible speaks against the use of Astrology and refers to astrologers as false saviors who offer no help. **"Let now the astrologers, those who prophesy by the stars, those who predict by the new moons, stand up and save you from what will come upon you. Behold, they have become like stubble...they cannot deliver themselves from the power of the flame."** (Isaiah 47:13-14)

Scripture shows that this practice is a type of prophecy because it is used to predict the future. The person uses the information to guide his choices, aligning himself with the prediction. Astrology is a way to "see ahead" through false principles and familiar spirits. But those people who use this means of prophecy to guide their life will someday meet Christ whom they attempted to avoid and will hear Him say, "Depart from Me, I never knew you!"

FREEMASONRY

Another institution that has its origin in the value system of Babylon and exemplifies man's propensity to be "climbers" rather than "followers" is the order of the Masonic Lodge, otherwise known as Masons or Freemasonry. This secret men's society, meaning that they hold closed meetings, is based upon religious rites, vows and charitable works in the community. Even though born-again Christians involve themselves with Masonic groups, the tenets of this religion do not align with the doctrines of the Christian faith and cannot be combined.

Like so many other spiritual groups, the Masons hold that they promote all religions and faiths with the understanding that there is only one God, but many ways to Him. "The Masonic claim that it truly unites all religions is evaluated."[19] cites John Ankerberg and John Weldon in their research of Masonic indoctrination. This is one of the factors that makes this organization so appealing to men. The Constitution of the Freemasons was changed to incorporate religious tolerance and language that was more all-encompassing. "A Mason is obliged by his tenure, to obey the Moral Law...now thought more expedient only to oblige them to that religion in which all men agree... that is, to be good men and true or men of honor and honesty; by whatever denominations or persuasions they may be distinguished..."[20] This is interpreted and accepted as saying that there is one God who created the world and that He is the Father of all humankind, making all men brothers. A secret brotherhood bonds men together and galvanizes friendships through a spiritual platform.

Albert Pike, one of the foremost authorities within the organization, wrote a defining code book for Masonry called *Morals and Dogma*. In it he states, "We belong to no one creed or school. In all religions, there is a basis of truth, in all there is pure morality...She (Masonry) invites all men of all religions to enlist under her banner."[21] Pike goes on to name great reformers, teachers and lawgivers such as Buddha, Moses, Confucius and Jesus. This all-inclusive faith exemplifies universalism.

The problem with this belief is that Jesus of the Bible says that He is the exclusive, one and only way to God. **"Jesus said to him, 'I am the way, and the truth, and the life; no one comes to the Father, but through Me.'" (John 14:6)** We can see that the creed of Masons and the claims

---

19 *The Secret Teachings of the Masonic Lodge,* P. 8
20 *Idiot's Guide to Freemasonry*, P. 203
21 *Fast Facts*, P. 311, P. 81

of Christ most certainly conflict. There are also other discrepancies to show that Masonry is a false religion.

Masons avow that all men from all religions are brothers and that they approach God on the basis of morality and good works.[22] Masonry teaches that entry into Heaven is acquired by works and self-improvement. "By it, he was constantly reminded of purity of life and that rectitude of conduct so necessary to his gaining admission into the Celestial Lodge above…"[23] Through a subjective philosophy where no standard is offered, individual Masons are free to determine their own interpretation of moral conduct and carry on the good works that they think will be sufficient to access the heavenly gates.

But once again, the Bible denounces this system of subjective morals and works. **"For by grace you have been saved through faith; and that not of yourselves, it is a gift of God; not as a result of works, that no one should boast." (Ephesians 2:8-9)** Biblical faith is belief in the work of Jesus on the Cross for our sins as the way to enter into God's presence. We had no part in it and we did not invent this way. God offers salvation as a free gift to those who are willing to believe the right things about Him.

Cult expert Ed Decker wrote in his book *Fast Facts* that there are over 4 million members in the United States with 15,300 lodges. He says that most Masons get into the organization for business or social reasons while others see philanthropic works as a way to get involved with the community. Masons pride themselves on the charitable works that they do such as Shriners' Circus, orphanages, hospitals and other enterprises.

Even so, this does not make up for the mystical occult rituals that go on behind closed doors. The community

---

22 *Fast Facts*, P. 80
23 *The Secret Teachings of the Masonic Lodge, P. 84*

projects disguise the occult practices to make them seem respectable. Men are drawn to the mysterious rituals and the thrill of being part of a secret brotherhood. "Masonry is an introduction into the occult in that it encourages the Mason to pursue its 'esoteric truths.' You will find that the ritual is but the beginning of what can be a tremendous spiritual and philosophical experience."[24]

The most obvious characteristic of Freemasonry that puts this organization in the category of "climbers" is the various steps that initiates must go through and are encouraged to progress "up the ladder." "All Masons unite in declaring it to be a system of morality, by the practice of which its members may advance their spiritual interest and mount the theological ladder from the lodge of earth to the Lodge in Heaven."[25] Masons advance through steps in ceremony and service. Legends about the rebuilding of Solomon's Temple have men focusing on mystical folklore of this esoteric temple. They refer to God as "The Great Architect" and say that they are His builders.

Just like climbing the ancient ziggurat, Masons advance in degrees either through the Scottish Rite or the York Rite. The highest ranking officiate who presides over the members of the Lodge is referred to as "The Worshipful Master." Through various non-Christian confessions, blood oaths and rites, men go "up the ladder," providing them with a sense of advancement and personal achievement.

All told, this organization creates a false priesthood that has men participating in building a make-believe tabernacle on a global scale. "It refers to itself as a 'Holy Empire' whose mission is 'to dispel darkness.'"[26] Again, false reli-

---

24 *The Secret Teachings of the Masonic Lodge*, P. 224
25 Ibid, P. 11
26 *Ibid*, P. 33

gions give people the opportunity to escape God's real purposes for them by busying themselves with meaningless spiritual practices. Those who have believed in the claims of the Masonic Lodge as their way of salvation will someday come to Jesus saying, "Lord, Lord, we did good works and cast out darkness in your Name!" and Jesus will refuse them entry, saying, "Depart from Me, I never knew you!"

REIKI

Let's look at another practice that produces false healing miracles done in the name of God with intentions to do good. This is the holistic healing practice of Reiki, which in Japanese means "Universal Life Force Energy."[27] Reiki is a practice of laying on of hands by channeling healing energy into the mind, body and emotions of patients.

This healing practice first began by a dean of a Christian college in Japan in the mid-1800's. Dr. Mikoa Usui was challenged by his students why miraculous healings were not more evident if the Bible was to be taken literally. Dr. Usui pursued those questions by coming to America and attending theological seminary at the University of Chicago.

Afterwards, he returned to Japan and also turned to the teachings of Buddha at several Buddhist monasteries. He eventually received "empowerment" after a 21 day fast and meditation in the Buddhist tradition. He began to perform healing "miracles" on himself and then went on to lay hands on the sick and the destitute. He eventually formulated and taught a method which became the current practice of Reiki.

---

27 *Empowerment Through Reiki*, P. 17

By combining the findings of Eastern religions with Christian sounding morals, he initiated the "Five Principles of Reiki." These religious ideas are meant to clear the practitioner's life and allow for a greater measure of healing power. The five principles are as follows: 1) Live in gratitude 2) Do not worry 3) Do not be angry 4) Do honest work 5) Show love and respect for every living thing. Supposedly by following these principles every day and learning how to release healing energy through the laying on of hands, people can once again do the healing miracles of Christ. "With the keys, the practitioner actually forms a 'bridge' between himself and the healee, so that energy can then be drawn as needed."[28]

The problem is that Reiki is not a Christ-centered practice. It is another "climber" religious sect that has its students advancing from First to Second to Third Degree as Reiki Masters. "Reiki is divided into three degrees. In Reiki I, the attunement itself heals physical level diseases in the person who receives it...Reiki I healing sessions are primarily for self-healing."[29]

Practitioners derive their power or energy from crystals, inner guides, angels, meditation and other traditions of "enlightenment" that have their origins in Buddhist religion. This is another all-encompassing spirituality that embraces all religions. "The teachings of all the great religions have many similarities, indeed some Christians, Muslims, or Jews are better Buddhists than some Buddhists, and vice-versa! It all comes down to the individual and his or her relationship with herself, himself, God, Buddha, Allah or whatever that person believes in...Whatever your spiritual path, or path of personal

---

28 *Empowerment Through Reiki*, P. 73
29 *Essential Reiki*, P. 17

growth, Reiki can enrich it and bring you closer to your full potential as a human being."[30]

Even though people have experienced healings, relief from pain and chronic illness through Reiki treatments, the flow of energy and "light" that is channeled through the Reiki practitioners is not the work of the Holy Spirit. "In doing healing sessions, the Reiki III Master experiences a further increase in her ability to channel healing energy."[31] The "energy" flow comes from people tapping into the demonic realm. Regardless of how many people received these healing miracles, this practice stems from ancient occultic arts and not from Christ Himself.

If these workers of false miracles do not have the Son of God at work in their lives by the power of the Holy Spirit, then they will not have eternal life. **"He who has the Son has the life; he who does not have the Son of God does not have the life." (1 John 5:12)** These workers of Reiki will be the people who will come to Christ saying, "We did miracles in your Name." Once again, Jesus will discount their works and say to them, "Depart from Me, I never knew you."

THE ATONEMENT

Christian belief holds that God is not a Universal Life Force but instead a Heavenly Father. He is not a "power" to have, but a Person to know. God's power is not separate from His personhood and He makes it clear that we can only come to know Him after the offense of our sin has been cleared through personal acceptance of the blood sacrifice of Jesus Christ.

---

30 *Reiki For Beginners*, P. XXI
31 *Essential Reiki*, P. 18

The one distinguishing element of doctrine that separates Christianity from all other beliefs is the requirement of coming into God's presence through the blood of the Lamb, which is the atoning sacrifice of Jesus. The question comes up as to why God requires a blood sacrifice to come into His presence. *Systematic Theology* author Wayne Grudem makes this sobering statement that puts things into perspective before he goes on to explain this doctrine. "Was there any other way for God to save human beings than by sending his Son to die in our place? Before answering this question, it is important to realize that it was not necessary for God to save any people at all. When we appreciate that **'God did not spare the angels when they sinned, but cast them into hell and committed them to pits of nether gloom to be kept until judgment.' (2 Peter 2:4)**, then we realize that God could have also chosen with perfect justice to have left us in our sins awaiting judgment. So in this sense the atonement was not absolutely necessary."[32]

At Gethsemane we hear Jesus praying to the Father this infamous prayer, **"My Father if it is possible, let this cup pass from Me; yet not as I will, but as Thou wilt." (Matthew 26:39)** Sometimes this is interpreted as the human side of Jesus hesitating to go to His death on the Cross knowing how brutal it will be for Him. But that was not what was happening because the author of Hebrews states that, **"for the joy set before Him, endured the Cross." (Hebrews 12:2)** Jesus was not trying to dissuade the Father from carrying out His mission.

More likely, Jesus was certifying that His death was the only way for people to come back into God's presence. Even though the disciples were groggy from sleep, He knew that the Holy Spirit would bring His words to the

---

32 *Systematic Theology*, P. 569

remembrance of the Gospel writers. Jesus wanted scripture to say forever that, because the Father did not remove the cup of suffering and bloody death from Jesus, then Jesus' death was absolutely necessary and the only legitimate way back to God. Therefore, the atonement was essential.

The atonement was foreshadowed in the beginning. God chose not to allow Satan's temptation of Adam and Eve to sway Him from His desire to tabernacle with men. Let's go back to that scene and see what God did. In Genesis 3, God confronts Adam about his disobedience and then passes fair judgment on the serpent. **"On your belly shall you go, and dust you shall eat all the days of your life; and I will put enmity between you and the woman and between your seed and her seed; He shall bruise you on the head and you shall bruise him on the heel." (Genesis 3:14-15)** He announced the atonement of Christ who would receive a bloody blow to cover Adam's offense. But Christ would deliver the final fatal blow to Satan after He leads a train of captives out of the bonds of sin. During the time between this announcement and its fulfillment, God would put a holy hatred of sin into the hearts of the offspring of the woman to distinguish the new race of man that He brings forth out of the old. This race of re-created people will take a stand for God against sin and Satan.

Let's talk about the consequences of Adam's sin. The word "sin" in Greek means "to miss the mark" as with an archer aiming for a target and missing the bulls eye center. In the spiritual context, it refers to a moral failure of a life veering off course and missing the high standard of God's perfect will. As a result, there is a gap, a breach or a separation between our fallen human nature that misses the mark of God's holy nature. An encounter with Him in this state is not possible because of the gulf that lies between us.

The fiber of our whole being has been infected and stained by sin. It is not just a matter of what we do or don't do that is wrong, but the way that we *are* that is wrong. Because of the knowledge that Satan offered our first parents, the whole human race has been tainted by the same arrogant rebellious reasoning that Satan himself operates in. Sin has made us defiled, depraved and defiant. Our whole self resists the ways of God in preference to the ways of self.

Sin is actually an act of insanity. For the creature to defiantly stand up to the Creator and say, "No, I refuse to do what you say!" is absolute madness. That we would be so headstrong about governing our own selves without God's involvement is utter chaos and insanity. Our self-reliant "freedom" is actually the path to our self-contained imprisonment.

Fortunately, God has not left us in our plight to right this horrendous wrong by ourselves. We simply cannot do it. Sin has gained power over us, we are stuck in it and we need someone more powerful to extract us. Sin has mastered us as a race because we have gone the way of Cain and refused God's warning. Sin controls us, it feeds us, it fuels our desires and speaks to us every day. The Apostle Paul realized his predicament and cried out, **"Wretched man that I am! Who will save me from the body of this death?" (Romans 7:24)**

As Christians, we depart from every other religion because we have chosen to believe in someone who has paid the price to redeem us from our slavery to sin. **"To Him who loves us, and released us from our sins by His blood…" (Revelation 1:5)** God gave us His Son Jesus, who He alluded to at the time of the Fall, as the perfect atoning sacrifice for our sin. At that time, the only acceptable way to enter back into God's presence was through animal sacrifice. That animal sacrifice pointed to Christ as man's ultimate sacrifice for sin.

Let's try to understand the justice of the atonement. All sin is an offense against God because He did not create us this way. Due to wrong beliefs, His workmanship was spoiled. He also created us specifically for relationship with Him, but that sacred union was broken. A dastardly crime was committed and the perpetrator must be held accountable in the courts of God's perfect justice.

Conscience tells us that wrong doing must be punished in order to clear the offense. When a crime is cleared through due punishment, then justice is served and satisfied. The debt of the perpetrator must be dealt with. God warned Adam that his disobedience would be punishable by death because it was a criminal act to disobey Almighty God. The first couple knew who God was and knew what He said. Yet, they chose to listen to Satan and threw all of creation into a downward spiral of death and dying. The debt of this catastrophic offense had to be paid!

God's provision of putting an animal to death instead of Adam temporarily covered or paid for Adam's offense. Adam and Eve wore the animal hides as proof that a substitute life had been taken on their behalf. Carrying through with this same requirement of atonement, Israel sacrificed goats and bulls daily as a temporary covering until the permanent payment was exacted by Christ once and for all. **"And inasmuch as it is appointed for men to die once and after this comes judgment, so Christ also, having been offered once to bear the sins of many, shall appear a second time for salvation without reference to sin to those who eagerly await Him."** (Hebrews 9:27-28) God allowed the substitutionary death of Jesus to act as the payment for the offense of Adam's race so that people could be cleared if they choose to accept the atonement.

We are told to fix our eyes on Jesus, always looking to Him who made atonement for us. **"...fixing our eyes on Jesus the author and finisher of our faith..." (Hebrews 12:2)** Jesus went to the Cross to be our sin-bearer with assured pleasure knowing that, through His death, people would be able to know the Father just as He knows Him. He gladly paid the price to open up the one way for man to have relationship with God once more. Because of the shed blood of Jesus, we can enter into God's presence with confidence and deep gratitude.

We can approach God knowing that He is pleased when we leave sin behind, accept Christ's death on our behalf and live our new life to the glory of God. He lets us know His pleasure with inner assurance and renewed power. Through repentance, we receive the knowledge of true righteousness which is the perfection of Christ for us.

Although God indicts us, He also defends us. His goal is to break the power of sin and self-will without crushing the person. He wants to release us, not condemn us. No matter how much sin we see in ourselves, we still have hope that God's love for us and extended mercy is greater than our hearts. All we have to do is say, "Yes" to Him.

We don't have to fear the words "I never knew you" if we have had a valid experience of knowing God by accepting His provision for us. Those who come to God by the atoning blood of Christ will hear this: **"Well done, good and faithful servant...enter into the joy of your master." (Matthew 25:21)** This eternal security is based upon relationship with God rather than religious speculations about Him.

Let's look at our right response to the atonement and also an obstacle to biblical faith that interferes with tabernacle.

CHAPTER FOUR

SANCTIFICATION VERSUS SELF-RIGHTOUSNESS

No matter what practices we have been involved in, God always offers people a turning point to repent and make a change. If the road away from God is pride and disobedience, then the road back is humility and obedience. The journey back to sanity begins when we decide that God is right and we have been wrong. The Bible says that the angels in Heaven throw a party when just one "climber" stops trying, turns to God and starts trusting. **"I tell you that in the same way, there will be more joy in heaven over one sinner who repents…" (Luke 15:7)**

The good news is that we have a Savior who paid the penalty for sin and obtained the forgiveness of God on our behalf forevermore. The only thing that God requires of us is to believe and receive this gift. This is the saving grace that God offers that takes us off the treadmill of trying by our own efforts to somehow reach God. Through Jesus, God has reached us. All we have to do is stop resisting Him and start resting in Him.

For those who accept God's terms of the relationship, Christ has made the provision for us to be united with our holy God and live in peaceful co-existence with Him. Christ has reconciled us to God and made it possible for us to be reinstated to that high and holy place that Adam once knew. Through a simple act of repentance, we can be joined with God by the indwelling Holy Spirit. **"For He Himself is our peace, who made both groups into one, and broke down the barrier of the dividing wall…that in Himself He might make the two into one new man, thus establishing peace." (Ephesians 2:14-15)**

SANCTIFICATION

First and foremost, God has saved us for Himself. After our salvation encounter, God will employ an ongoing saving work called "sanctification" which is meant to remove any barriers of sin that remain hostile towards Him. The indwelling Holy Spirit reveals specific sins that are offensive to God's holy presence and supplies us the power to overcome those deceptive ways. God doesn't want to just forgive us of our sins, but also heal us from the devastating effects that sin has had upon us and our relationships.

To "sanctify" means "to set apart, to make holy, to purify and to make free or separate from sin." **"And such were some of you; but you were washed, but you were sanctified, but you were justified in the name of the Lord Jesus Christ, and in the Spirit of our God." (1 Corinthians 6:11)** This is a necessary work if we are going to pursue a vital relationship with our Holy God and get to know Him more and more. We must cooperate with the ongoing work of repentance when the Holy Spirit brings conviction. He is actually leading us into a fuller measure of God's presence, which is what we should want. The Holy Spirit cleanses the human temple, making it a suitable habitation for God's inner presence. **"For just as you once presented your members as slaves to impurity and to greater and greater iniquity, so now present your members as slaves to righteousness for sanctification."** **(Romans 6:19)** In Christ, the place where we tabernacle with God is in our hearts. **"Do you not know that you are a temple of God, and that the Spirit of God dwells in you?"** **(1 Corinthians 3:16)**

The purpose of sanctification is for us to willingly quit specific habits such as the love of sin, the love of self and wrong relationships that tempt us to do ungodly acts. In order to make a distinct people set apart for His purposes, He must make us holy. **"And also by all who had joined them and separated themselves from the pollutions of the nations of the land to worship the Lord, the God of Israel." (Ezra 6:21)**

Prophetic author Rick Joyner explains this process of separation in the context of creation. "The Lord's first act of creation was to bring forth light. The very next thing He did was separate the light from the darkness. There can be no cohabitation between light and darkness. When the Lord re-creates a man and he is born-again, He immediately begins to separate the light from the darkness in his life."[33] Even though we appear to be the same people outwardly, inwardly through the careful re-working of our thoughts, ideas and core beliefs, we are changed to resemble Christ. God shines His search light within us to discover the depths of lies that we have accepted and brings them to our understanding. We then have a conscious choice to either ignore or accept the light of truth that God has shown us.

Hopefully, our love for God, fear of God and obedience to God will win out as we choose to refuse sin. If we

33 *There Were Two Trees In The Garden,* P. 12

know the benefits of ongoing repentance then the decision will be much easier for us to make. Knowing that there is great value in holiness and godly living, we will welcome this work. **"For the grace of God has appeared, bringing salvation to all, training us to renounce impiety and worldly passions, and in the present age to live our lives that are self-controlled, upright and godly, while we wait for the blessed hope and manifestation of the glory of our great God and Savior Jesus Christ. He is who gave himself for us that he might redeem us from all iniquity and purify for himself a people of his own who are zealous for good deeds." (Titus 2:11-14)** This is godly character that God values so much.

There are three main benefits of sanctification. First, God wants to make us "clean" by removing all moral filth and defilement from us. Sin makes us dirty even to the point of feeling uncomfortable to live with ourselves. We loathe ourselves for the horrible things that we do and say. We know that our behavior is wrong. But until God corrects us, we can't do anything about the way we are. God helps us by His power to walk in human dignity rather than human depravity. He enables us to distinguish the gray areas to clearly see right from wrong. In this way we can have an honest life of integrity because we know that we are living the right way.

Secondly, God wants us to live "clear." He gives us a new clarity to our thinking and perception. God brings definition through His Word and heals our mind as truth finds a home in our heart. When our mind is renewed, the fog of confusion lifts and we see life with an alert, hopeful perspective. **"God does not give us a spirit of fear but one of love, power and a sound mind." (2 Timothy 1:7)** He also sharpens our discernment, which is the ability to distinguish right from wrong, so that we can have God's wisdom and insight into spiritual matters. **"I have directed** you in the way of wisdom; I have led you in upright paths." (Proverbs 4:11)

Thirdly, sanctification is the way that we are able to draw "close" to God. **"Draw near to God and He will draw near to you. Cleanse your hands, you sinners; and purify your hearts, you double-minded." (James 4:8)** Our motive for repentance is to draw close to a fearfully holy, yet wonderfully personal God. As a result, we will become effective in prayer and have power for any Christian service that we do. The smallest saint can move mile high mountains if he has Heaven shining down on him because of right living. **"Therefore, confess your sins to one another, and pray for one another, so that you may be healed. The effective prayer of a righteous man can accomplish much." (James 5:16)**

God makes us clean, clear and close through the process of sanctification. Probably one of the most important aspects of this work is the ability to understand how we have answered the call of Babylon, serving the world instead of God. He enables us to stop heeding its voice in order to come and join the purposes of God. **"How Babylon has become an object of horror among the nations!...Come out of her my people!" (Jeremiah 51:41, 45)** We must stop resisting the will of God, stop ignoring His voice and choose to serve Him alone. We forsake dreams of fame and fortune, spending our time on foolish pleasure seeking. We are not to be "married" to the world, chasing it like a smitten lover. **"Do not love the world, nor the things in the world. If anyone loves the world, the love of the Father is not in him." (1 John 2:15)** Sanctification helps us shift our affections off of this world system and its corrupted desires. Our love is purified by higher goals because God enlightens us as to what is truly valuable. **"And the world is passing away, and also its lusts; but the one who does the will of God abides forever." (1 John 2:17)**

The main reason that God wants to move our affections off of material possessions is to keep us out of idolatry. At the time of Israel, worshiping pagan gods became the nation's downfall. We see the withdrawal of the presence of God from among them due to the idolatry that offended God's presence so greatly. **"This occurred because the people of Israel had sinned against the Lord their God…They had worshiped other gods…" (2 Kings 17:7, 20)**

Idolatry is anything that interferes with our love for God. An idol is something or someone that we love and value more than Him. It could be anything that our heart lays hold of and clutches to itself to comfort or empower us. We emotionally attach ourselves to a created thing and say, "This supports me. I need this to live." We think that it will take the uncertainty out of life and that, as long as we have it, we will be safe because we have something to hold onto. An idol seems to define us and delineate us; we somehow find our identity in it. It gives substance to our being because we are afraid to stand alone. So we fill the "hole in our heart" with created things instead of God because we can't stand the emptiness that we feel. Again, we were never ever meant to be joined emotionally to created things in this way. **"Therefore, beloved, flee from idolatry." (1 Corinthians 10:14)**

The reason why God hates idolatry is because we become so bound in our desire for created things that we are not free to pursue relationship with Him. The two loves conflict. God is very jealous for us and wants our heart to beat solely for Him. **"You shall have no other gods before Me. You shall not worship them or serve them; for I, the Lord your God, am a jealous God…" (Exodus 20:3-5)** With jealous zeal, the Holy Spirit comes to disprove and eradicate other loves that compete with the love of God. He helps us fall out to love with self-seeking and become disenchanted with the mystical lure of this world and its illusions of grandeur.

Christian maturity is achieved through sanctification. We grow up to accept the commands and desires of God, realizing that He has called us to adulthood to bear responsibilities for the sake of others. We must learn to change our orientation off of self and onto God. Before knowing God, all we knew was our own self. But when we turned to God, we saw Jesus beckoning us to come follow Him. **"... But whenever a man turns to the Lord, the veil is taken away." (2 Corinthians 3:16)** He helps us to straighten up and turn fully towards Him by getting our focus off of self. He wants us to stand before Him as faithful, whole adult persons rather than as crippled, unruly children.

When we see the kingdom through spiritual eyes, we then re-orient ourselves to conform to Christ who becomes our focal point. Our scope has changed and our approach to life is different because the kingdom has a different value system that the world. **"Seek first the kingdom of God and His righteousness." (Matthew 6:33)** New priorities take the place of old interests.

The "city" where God dwells is Zion and He establishes that dwelling place wherever His is worshiped fully and His commandments are obeyed. **"Zion shall be redeemed by justice, and those in her who repent by righteousness." (Isaiah 1:27)** This is the atmosphere that is conducive to God's presence where He can inhabit and remain. The call goes out from Zion to come to the Lord and worship Him. Through sanctification, we begin to know the pleasure of giving God worship. It is only though sanctification that our hearts are released to be free to worship God and ascend to that high and holy place where He dwells in order to tabernacle with Him. **"In days to come the mountain of the Lord's house shall be established as the highest of mountains, and shall be raised above the hills; all the nations** shall stream to it. Many peoples shall come and say, 'Come, let us go up to the mountain of the Lord...'" (Isaiah 2:1)

SELF-RIGHTEOUSNESS

We understand that people receive salvation through Jesus Christ by no effort of their own. Christianity is not a "works" faith that teaches people to achieve upgrading levels of spirituality by their activities. The invitation to have a restored relationship with God is a free gift that He provided out of willingness to have us back in His arms. The truth of redemption must cut us to the heart as we appreciate the investment that God has made to buy us back. **"It is by grace that you have been saved, through faith; and that not of yourselves, it is the gift of God; not as a result of works, that no one should boast." (Ephesians 2:8-9)** As a result of this compelling, life-changing message, we should want to draw near to the One who laid down His life for us.

Sanctification is the only reasonable response to our new life in Christ because we realize what a costly gift it is. Our own sin produced the barrier that at one time kept us far away from God. Once we accept the remedy, why would we want sin anymore? Why would we resist the process that the Holy Spirit immediately begins upon conversion? Many times people testify of instant deliverance and healing from destructive habits such as smoking, drinking or taking drugs when they meet Christ and receive Him as their Savior. With so much delivering power available to us, why would we keep the sin that the Savior died to dispose of?

In the Book of Romans, the Apostle Paul makes a painstaking case to early Christians to value their new life in Christ by refusing sin and, in fact, understand the power that they have to stay free. He explained the dynamics of our interaction with the indwelling Holy Spirit to keep us away from the enemy of sin that was our downfall. Very quickly in his letter, Paul cites the opposing attitude that stops people from pursuing the righteous life that God has revealed through the Gospel. He pinpoints the inner motives of "climbers" who still hold to the dream of being seen and applauded by men. **"...but to those who are selfishly ambitious and do not obey the truth, but obey unrighteousness, wrath and indignation." (Romans 2:8)**

Even though man cannot boast about the salvation that God provides because he had nothing to do with producing it, some people will cling to self-righteousness for performance sake. Even though the two beliefs are incompatible, people can trick their minds into thinking that, yes they are sinners saved by grace, but their sin wasn't that bad because basically they are good people. Many times people are brought up with a religious background that teaches salvation through good works. They have a very hard time moving from "I try" to simply "I trust." Even though we have done nothing to earn or deserve God's free gift of salvation, we do not like to be found devoid of doing. Self-righteousness has us chafing at the thought of such empty-handedness. Our innate arrogance often shows up here as an effective stumbling block. We simply choose not to refine our beliefs because the offense to self becomes so unbearable. Even though we read, **"there is none righteous, not even one; there is none who does good, there is not even one." (Romans 3:10)** we still think that we are the exception by mentally removing ourselves and deciding that we are not really that bad.

I have personally met people who have accepted Christ as Lord and Savior, yet balk at reading the Book of Romans in the Bible because its teaching so completely trashes their claim of coming to God by good works. The self-humiliation and denial of their own abilities was too much for them to bear. This mentality has people starting and then effectively stopping sanctification due to self-righteousness. Let me go on to explain how this attitude halts the flow of the Holy Spirit and interrupts His attempts to take us to tabernacle.

Self-righteousness puts us in an analytical mindset where we mentally classify so-called "good people" and "bad people." Of course, we place ourselves in the category of "good people" which gives us the option to look down upon everyone else. Based on judging, people look around to compare themselves with those who are "bad" in order to validate this type of reasoning. The knowledge of good and evil blinds us from seeing our own personal evil by ignoring it, making excuses and protecting ourselves by reasoning our sins away.

If we dwell on the faults of others, then somehow we think that it makes us look better by comparison. Self-righteous people always focus on the short-comings of others. They tell themselves, "At least I am not as bad as that person!" If we spot others who are astray, we somehow think that makes us above reproach and in better standing with God.

When we become disgusted by the moral failure of others, it produces a smug "holier than thou" attitude. It is our way of celebrating ourselves at the expense of someone else's weakness. Jesus cited the propensity of man to celebrate his own "goodness" and look down upon his brother's "badness" with the parable of the Pharisee and the tax collector. **"The Pharisee stood and was praying thus to himself, 'God, I thank Thee that I am not like other people; swindlers, unjust, adulterers, or even like this tax-gatherer. I fast twice a week; I pay tithes of all that I get.'" (Luke 18:11-12)** Blinded by the self-righteous sensations of all he was doing, the Pharisee missed seeing the grace of God that he actually needed. A hypocrite is someone who requires faultless behavior in others, yet refuses to impose the same standard upon himself.

Although this was a parable and not a real situation, Jesus gave this example to portray two actual reactions that people have to their awareness of sin and human failure. One way has us celebrating our own goodness in comparison with everyone else based upon the religious activities that we are doing. The other has us bowing before God in complete humility, realizing our brokenness and crying out for His mercy.

The main problem with self-righteousness is that we rise up in our thoughts and permit ourselves to become judge and jury over the lives of others. In our self-satisfaction, we convince ourselves that everyone else has the problem, never us. When we come to the conclusion, "I am fine just the way I am and everyone else needs to change," then we significantly halt the healing that God wants through sanctification. We become so secure in our form of righteousness that we never avail ourselves to the real change that God wants to accomplish. **"There are those who are pure in their own eyes yet are not cleansed of their filthiness. There are those-how lofty are their eyes, how high their eyelids lift!" (Proverbs 30:12-13)** This verse says that there are those who are so self-righteous that they pretend to be shocked at other people's sin as if they would never think of doing such a thing. They flatter themselves by disconnecting from their own condition and never allow God to remove their own impurities. They are too busy being put-off by the sins of others.

When we act as self-righteous judges, we may even be happy when we see the "bad people" getting the punishment that we think they deserve. Many people today hold to a supposed law of "karma" or a system of justice that says, "What goes around comes around." This belief in karma is a non-Christian idea that is rooted in Hinduism and Buddhism teachings, saying that a person's mental and physical deeds, good or bad, will determine the consequences of his life, rebirth or reincarnation.[34] People gain a selfish satisfaction in the demise of others who should "get what they deserve." We allow ourselves much self-righteous anger when we become so adamant about punishing others. We want to see them pay and pay and pay! Because we are unable to separate the sin from the sinner in our minds, we hold people in religious contempt that fills us with a hating, critical spirit.

Self-righteousness is only a smoke screen putting off the true personal repentance and holiness that God wants. It is an inaccurate judgment of one's self under a wrong light. We actually need God's light to rightly judge our inner attitudes. Then we can see our own heart that harbors haughty pride and arrogance.

Fortunately God does not view people as "good" and "bad" people but as believers and non-believers, righteous and unrighteous based upon their decision to accept His Gospel and obey. **"And it will come about that whoever calls on the name of the Lord will be delivered." (Joel 2:32)** This is the doctrine that we should adopt. Otherwise, we can effectively offend the Holy Spirit with our judgmental attitudes and halt tabernacle.

Since we have been saved by unmerited grace, then we always want to stay on the side of grace by wanting God's mercy and favor to come to others, no matter how much we see they have sinned. Even for those who we deem to be the deepest, direst sinners, we must take the position that all sin is an offense against God, not against us.

---

34 *Metaphysical Encyclopedia*, P. 312

"Against Thee only, I have sinned, and done what is evil in Thy sight." (Psalm 51:4)

God made the provision to forgive all sin by the death of His Son, so it doesn't really matter what we think or the revenge that we want. All that matters is the truth that Jesus paid the debt of all human sin. There is absolutely no sin that is outside or beyond the reach of the Cross. God is willing and able to forgive and cleanse the most notorious, despicable acts that people have done. This is the amazing grace that God offers that is celebrated and sung about.

In order to do intercession, we should want mercy for others. We need to have right motives as we pray. **"For though the Lord is exalted, he regards the lowly, but the haughty he knows from far away." (Psalm 138:6)** We are called as followers to believe in God's mercy and intercede on behalf of sinners, just as Jesus now does for us. There is a mind-boggling level of mercy and grace that God is willing to pour out upon people to make them aware of His presence and His glorious salvation. **"The Lord is not slow about His promise, as some count slowness but is patient toward you, not wishing for any to perish but all to come to repentance." (2 Peter 3:9)** If God says that He is willing for all men to come to repentance, then we must believe and hold to this vast promise by actually wanting this to happen in our world.

Sanctification allows believers to be more effective in prayer to actually see this type of display of mercy and grace take place. It clears our lives of unbelief and guilt so that we can accept the outpouring that the Holy Spirit wants to do. The Bible says that we can come boldly before the throne of grace. **"Let us therefore draw near with confidence to the throne of grace, that we may receive mercy and may find grace to help in time of need." (Hebrews 4:16)** The reason we can approach God so confidently is because our conscience is cleansed of self-righteous anger and critical hatred of others. Instead, we come before God to seek His help and mercy on behalf of those who do not know Him. We come to Him with gratitude in our hearts, knowing that He freely forgave us and in turn, we seek His forgiveness for others.

Those who take the journey of sanctification are released to a closer friendship with God and will begin to understand His heart to draw all men to Himself. **"For thus says the high and exalted one who lives forever, whose name is Holy: I dwell in the high and holy place, and also with those who are contrite and humble in spirit." (Isaiah 57:15)** It is this place of contrition, admitting our need of God's presence that we can tabernacle rightly to fulfill the holy vocation of God's priests. Let's go on to examine how the Lord employs sanctified believers as a holy priesthood before Him.

CHAPTER FIVE

the priesthood

In this chapter, we will look at the origin of the priesthood and find out God's standards for ministry in this capacity. Fulfilling this calling requires some self-discipline, but God gives us the anointing to make this vocation so satisfying that we will want to do it. **"Anoint them just as you anointed their father, so they may serve me as priests. Their anointing will be a priesthood that will continue for generations to come." (Exodus 40:15)**

The animal sacrifices that God required for the temporary atonement ceased with the one-time sacrifice of Christ. He became the perfect Lamb of God whose blood covers the Mercy Seat in Heaven on our behalf forever. Even so, the requirement of a holy priesthood ministering to the Lord was and is perpetual—ongoing from the time of Moses throughout eternity. **"Aaron was set apart, he and his descendants forever, to consecrate the most holy things, to offer sacrifices before the Lord, to minister before Him and pronounce blessings in His name forever." (1 Chronicles 23:13)** Reviewing the Old Testament Levitical priesthood, we can better envision the unceasing worship that we participate in to guard and protect God's presence.

At the time of Moses, the priesthood was a consecrated family of men who were called to interface with the holy presence of God—and live! In her book *Intimate Friendship With God,* Joy Dawson makes this statement, "I believe the most important part of God's character is His holiness. We will never understand the mercy of God until we have understood the holiness of God."[35] She explains that the other attributes of God's greatness, His love, His justice and His miraculous power are also very important. But it is His holiness that is constantly sung about in Heaven. "Yet God has chosen in His sovereignty that day and night living creatures are singing without ceasing, 'Holy, holy, holy, is the Lord God Almighty, who was and is and is to come.'…It must be that God in His infinite wisdom and knowledge sees holiness as the attribute above every other of His attributes of which all heaven and earth need to be constantly reminded."[36]

The holiness of God instills awe within us. His perfection penetrates us and diminishes all other attractions. Joy Dawson also makes this very provocative statement, "The beauty of the Lord Jesus comes from His holiness. When we gaze into the eyes of the Son of God, we see His eyes burn with the fire of holiness and with the fire of His love. Do you know what that does to us? It ruins us for the ordinary."[37] **"And I turned to see the voice that was speaking with me…And His head and His hair were white like white wool, like snow, and His eyes were like a flame of fire." (Revelation 1:12, 14)** The essence of the vocation of the priesthood is to value the presence of God above everything else. We must ask ourselves if we prepared to lose our appetite for the things of this world as we become mesmerized by His fiery beauty.

---

35 *Intimate Friendship With God,* P. 45
36 Ibid, P. 46
37 Ibid, P. 48

If so, then we must implement a new value system. We forsake the call of Babylon that incites us to compete for the fame and fortunes of this world and be rewarded by the attentions of men. **"If you return to the Almighty, you will be restored, if you remove unrighteousness from your tents, if you treat gold like dust, and gold of Ophir like the stones of the torrent bed, and if the Almighty is your gold and your precious silver, then you will delight yourself in the Almighty, and lift up your face to God." (Job 22:23-30)** We realize that money is not the answer for all of our problems. Giving money to people doesn't fix the broken places of their lives. The unhappiness and ills of society are rooted in deep places that money cannot reach. We have to move our trust off of the almighty dollar and onto Almighty God.

The Person of God and the power He exerts on our behalf is our only legitimate answer. In Him we have all that we need pertaining to real life. When we awaken to our need of God, then we will find our source of supernatural healing. The starting point is when we empty ourselves of opinions and mindsets about how to fix modern society and avail ourselves to what God says He wants to do. We need to re-evaluate the significance of the presence of God and insist that Immanuel is our single-most important possession. Everything else falls beneath having Him.

Those who see Immanuel as their answer and who wholeheartedly seek Him will have Him! **"And you, my son Solomon, know the God of your father, and serve him with single mind and willing heart; for the Lord searches every mind and understands every plan and thought. If you seek him, he will be found by you..." (1 Chronicles 28:9)** As mentioned before, God wants to dwell with man, be man's exclusive God and have a holy people for Himself. This has always been God's goal and

He will not be dissuaded despite man's bent towards rebellion.

The great proof of this in the Bible is the nation of Israel. Through amazing miraculous displays of power, God delivered the people of Israel out of bondage in Egypt that they might worship Him in the prescribed way. **"Although the whole earth is mine, you will be for me a kingdom of priests and a holy nation." (Exodus 19:5-6)**

The word of God was given to Moses to build a tabernacle or sanctuary in the desert in order to have a place where the glorious presence of God would actually meet and dwell with man. God proved how His plans would not be thwarted by the wrong choices of man through the tribe He chose to minister to Him. This is another one of those ironies in biblical history where God chooses the least likely family to redeem and exalt.

Levi was one of the sons of Jacob born to him by his wife Leah. Jacob, who was now called Israel, pronounced a blessing and prophesied over each one of his sons just before he died. Unfortunately, Levi's life of cruel unnecessary violence came to his father's remembrance and his blessing became a curse. **"Simeon and Levi are brothers; their swords are implements of violence. Let my soul not enter into their council; Let not my glory be united with their assembly; Because in their anger they slew men..." (Genesis 49:5-7)**

We can never underestimate God's ability to turn a curse into a blessing. He exhibits His willingness to bring near to Him those who have transgressed and are far off. God changed His mind about never being in the council of Levi or not allowing His glory to be united with his family because that is exactly what He did with the Levitical priesthood. When it came to choosing a tribe of Israel to be pent up and tabernacle with His presence, He reversed the curse and chose the tribe of Levi. As an example of true repentance, the tribe of Levi had the duty to stand before God and request God's mercy and forgiveness on behalf of the other tribes of Israel. **"Again the Lord spoke to Moses, saying, 'Now, behold I have taken the Levites from among the sons of Israel instead of the first-born, the first issue of the womb among the sons of Israel. So the Levites shall be Mine." (Numbers 3:12)** Of course this foreshadows the Savior who became a curse for us so that we might become the righteousness of God.

God gave the Levites the responsibility of maintaining the tabernacle, ministering before the Lord, making the animal sacrifices and physically moving the tent when the glory cloud of God's presence moved. God named Moses' brother Aaron to be in charge of the priesthood and to manage the duties of the priests.

Before we discuss the ministry of the Levites, let's take a brief look at the meeting place. After God spoke to Moses to give him The Ten Commandments and the various laws, God then gave Moses explicit directions to build a tent of meeting that would be conducive to God's holy presence. This would not only be a place of worship but also a place where God could speak to Moses and guide him as the nation's leader. From willing contributions collected from the Israelites, Moses assembled the materials, the gold, jewels and exquisitely made furnishings that would decorate the inside of the otherwise drab looking tent. Every part of the structure and design would symbolize the work of Christ. God required impeccable obedience on behalf of the people in order to represent the pattern of God's dwelling place in Heaven.

M.R. DeHaan, M.D. details the symbolism and meaning of each decoration in his timeless work *The Tabernacle.* "It was, therefore, a perfect replica of something which already existed before in heaven. The tabernacle was a type and a shadow of something with real substance...but of one thing we are sure, the tabernacle is a picture, a type and a shadow of the Lord Jesus Christ, where God meets man, and where deity and humanity meet in one person... Every detail of the tabernacle, therefore, points to some aspect of the person and work of our Savior."[38] God replicated the heavenly tabernacle in the midst of Israel for their worship of Him in the desert.

The tabernacle or tent of meeting became the portable sanctuary that would attract and "house" the presence of God on earth. Because Moses obeyed God's directions so thoroughly, God now had a place of His own design as it was in Heaven. As long as man obeyed His charge of prescribed worship, then God's presence was protected from the offense of man's sin and was comfortable enough to remain. **"On the day the tabernacle, the tent of the testimony, was set up, the cloud covered it. From evening till morning the cloud above the tabernacle looked like fire. That is how it continued to be; the cloud covered it and at night it looked like fire. Whenever the cloud lifted from above the tent, the Israelites set out; wherever the cloud settled, the Israelites encamped." (Numbers 9:15-17)**

The challenge to the nation of Israel was to learn God's ways and obey His directives in such a way that they would be able to maintain relationship with God to preserve and protect His presence with them. It was the manifest presence of God that made them distinct above all the other nations of the world. They had the Spirit of the Living God permeating their camp! Now that Israel had God's holy presence living among them, their job was to keep it.

God gave clear instructions to them on how to steward His presence through the daily sacrifices. Through the sacrifice of lambs, bulls and goats, the blood temporarily covered the sins of the people. **"Now this is what**

---

38 *The Tabernacle*, Introduction

you shall offer on the altar: two lambs a year old regularly each day. One lamb you shall offer in the morning, and the other lamb you shall offer in the evening…" (Exodus 29:38) Through the atonement, God's holy presence was preserved. The constant flow of blood was a reminder to the people of their sinful condition before a holy God. As long as the requirements of atonement were offered by the priests on behalf of the people, God and man could cohabitate the same vicinity. It was the responsibility of the Levites to keep the altar of the Mercy Seat covered with the sacrificial blood. But there were other priestly duties that God required in order to protect His presence from the offense of sin.

Besides the blood sacrifices, there were also burnt offerings and offerings of incense. God required that the fire on the altar be kept burning and never go out. This meant that the priests had to tend to the altar fires day and night. **"The fire on the altar shall be kept burning; it shall not go out. Every morning the priests shall add wood to it, lay out the burnt offering on it, and turn into smoke the fat pieces of well-being. A perpetual fire shall be kept burning on the altar; it shall not go out." (Leviticus 6:12-13)**

We find symbolism in this forever flame that the priests tended to. Not only does it speak of the diligence of the believer to tend to his own zeal for God and never allow it to flicker and die, but more importantly, it reminds us of God's fiery hatred of sin and His love and zeal for us that burns even stronger. Stephen F. Olford in his book *The Tabernacle, Camping Out With God,* explains the altar fire this way. "The fire pans suggest the zealousness of the Savior's cross work…Although the fire on the altar speaks of the wrath of God against sin, it also signifies the zeal, passion and love that burned in the Savior's heart to deal with the matter of sin and to accomplish man's redemption."[39]

Another type of service that the Levites performed was to stand before the Lord and pronounce blessings to Him continually. We can easily see that this type of constant confession of God's goodness in worship matches the ongoing reverence in Heaven. We have a God who deserves worship and the fruit of our lips should bring honor, blessings and exaltation unto Him. **"Aaron was set apart to consecrate the most holy things, so that he and his sons forever should make offerings before the Lord, and minister to Him and pronounce blessing in his name forever...And they shall stand every morning thanking and praising the Lord, and likewise at evening." (1 Chronicles 23:13, 30)** Here we see that one of the duties of the priests was to minister directly to the Lord, honoring Him as a Person and their welcomed guest. This is the ministry that became perpetual.

This idea may seem strange since we know that God is perfect and has no defects in character. Why would He need people to minister to Him through constant praise and adoration? This is a fascinating truth that really shows how personal and relational Almighty God is, that He would draw us to Himself in such a way. Because He is a Person, He enjoys closeness with us. He loves the appreciation that He receives when His power, protection and provision are recognized and hailed. We minister to the Lord and protect His emotions from man's scorn, indifference and ill-will. God allowed a designated circle of priests to use their lives in showing constant attention, desire and appreciation of Him. Praise and thanksgiving from man gives God pleasure. It satisfies His need, in a sense, to be valued and loved. God is love and, therefore,

---

39 *The Tabernacle, Camping Out With God*, P. 81

dwells in an atmosphere of love and gratitude. One of the key factors in protecting the presence of God is to give Him the attention, credit and thanksgiving that He unquestionably deserves. **"Come bless the Lord, all you servants of the Lord, who stand by night in the house of the Lord. Lift up your hands to the holy place, and bless the Lord. May the Lord, maker of heaven and earth, bless you from Zion." (Psalm 134:1-3)**

As a result of ministering to the Lord, the priests were then authorized to pronounce blessings in His name over the people. The ministry of the Levitical priests kept the entire nation of Israel in a state of blessing, protection and increase because of Immanuel. God's pleasure has tangible benefits for those who value His presence. God's goodness flows from His enjoyment of being in the midst of the people that He loves so much. The Levites pronounced blessings as evidence of God's care for the people who were the object of His love. **"At that time the Lord set apart the tribe of Levi to carry the ark of the covenant of the Lord, to stand before the Lord to minister and to pronounce blessings in his name, as they still do today." (Deuteronomy 10:8-9)**

We see this type of blessing pronounced over Hannah at the time of Eli the priest. Hannah went to the temple of the Lord and was in deep distress from her inability to bear children. Her emotional pain was so intense that all she could do was move her lips in prayer. Eli the priest observed her and thought she was drunk. He rebuked her for coming to the temple in a drunken state, but Hannah explained to him that she was in deep unspoken prayer. Acting in his priestly vocation, Eli pronounced a blessing upon her in accordance with his ministry to the people who came to the temple. **"Then Eli answered and said, 'Go in peace; and may the God of Israel grant your petition that you have asked of Him.'" (1 Samuel 1:17)**

Hannah left with her blessing and was no longer upset. In spite of Eli's insensitivity, the Lord touched Hannah with His presence. Soon afterwards, she had relations with her husband and she conceived. We can see that the priesthood had a vital ministry unto the Lord and also to the people who received the benefits of Immanuel.

Another privilege of the Levitical priesthood was to hear God speak. Of course the greatest example of God speaking to man as a friend was His humble servant Moses. **"When Moses went into the tent of meeting to speak with the Lord, he would hear the voice speaking to him from above the mercy seat that was on the ark of the covenant from between the two cherubim; thus it spoke to him."** **(Numbers 7:89)** Moses went into the tent of meeting to speak with the Lord "face to face."

God confirmed His endorsement and delegated authority to Moses before the people by a frightening display of His fiery presence at Mt. Sinai. God wanted the people to not only love and worship Him, but to also fear His terrible power. Moses was not devastated by such close proximity with God's thunder and fire because he had won God's friendship by his obedience, much like Noah and Abraham. **"And the Lord said to Moses, 'Behold, I shall come to you in a thick cloud, in order that the people may hear when I speak with you, and may also believe in you forever."** **(Exodus 19:9)**

It was in this setting of a smoking mountain, burning like a furnace and a loud trumpet blast that God announced to His friend His relentless desire to bless the whole earth with His presence through a consecrated people that would obey Him. God called the nation of Israel to become an extension and representation of God's heavenly kingdom. He charged them to corporately return to the high and holy place of co-habitation with God. **"Now then, if you will indeed obey My voice** and keep My covenant, then you shall be My own pos-session among all the peoples, for all the earth is Mine; and you shall be to Me a kingdom of priests and a holy nation." (Exodus 19:5-6)

God cast His ultimate vision through Moses and gave him specific laws for the people to follow. The Levitical priesthood was put in charge of enforcing those laws by teaching the people the Word of the Lord. They taught people God's standards for living, helping them to know the difference between what was holy and profane. **"Then you will know that I have sent this commandment to you, that my covenant may continue with Levi, says the Lord of Hosts…True instruction was in his mouth, and unright-eousness was not found on his lips; …for the lips of a priest should preserve knowledge, and men should seek instruction from his mouth; for he is the messenger of the Lord of Hosts." (Malachi 2:4-7)**

Israel learned the ways of God in the wilderness and kept God's presence through the ministry of the priest-hood although their honeymoon experience was tumul-tuous due to the people's constant rebellion. Several times God threatened to remove Himself from among them because of their chronic dissent. Horrified with the thought of losing God's presence, Moses stretched him-self out before the Lord, interceding on behalf of the peo-ple. Eventually, God successfully delivered Israel to her destination across the Jordan River to the Promised Land because of Moses' intercession.

After God's strong leaders Moses and Joshua died, the integrity of the priesthood broke down and threatened the presence of the Lord. Eventually, God stopped speaking to the priests as a sign of His displeasure, warning them to return to holiness. Hannah's deep distress in her barren-ness was God's way of stirring up their desire for the return of His Word. Out of her deep prayer, God provided Israel with an unwavering priest who powerfully and personally enforced God's ways. This was the effective ministry of Samuel. **"Now the sons of Eli were scoundrels; they had no regard for the Lord or the duties of the priests to the people...Thus the sin of the young men was very great in the sight of the Lord; for they treated the offerings of the Lord with contempt...And the boy Samuel grew up in the presence of the Lord."** (1 Samuel 2:12, 17) Similar to the relationship that God had with Moses, Samuel heard the voice of God clearly and communicated the current Word of the Lord to the people.

Sadly, Israel rebelled and rejected her God-given judge Samuel by demanding a king to lead her. God lamented to Samuel that the people were essentially rejecting the presence of God that they felt so powerfully through his priestly ministry. **"And the Lord said to Samuel, 'Listen to the voice of the people in regard to all they say to you, for they have not rejected you, but they have rejected Me from being king over them.'"** (1 Samuel 8:7) Refusing and resisting the immanent presence of God to pursue idolatry was the cause for Israel's downfall and failure to complete God's vision for the nation. Illicit worship of other gods offended and repelled the presence of God, driving Him away.

Over and over again God warned the leaders of Israel that, if they stopped obeying His voice and turned aside to worship foreign gods, they would greatly offend His presence and He would remove His Spirit from among them. The blessings, protection, power, health and divine provision that were part of the abiding presence of God were not guaranteed if God removed His Spirit from the land.

Even King Solomon, who so completely pleased the Lord with all he did to govern Israel rightly, seeking God for wisdom and then building a permanent temple for God's presence, was warned not to turn away lest he forfeit God's blessings from His presence. **"I have heard the prayer and plea you have made before me; I have consecrated this temple, which you have built, by putting my Name there forever. My eyes and my heart will always be there...But if you or your sons turn away from me and do not observe the commands and decrees I have given you and go off to serve other gods and worship them, then I will cut off Israel from the land I have given them and will reject this temple I have consecrated for my Name." (1 Kings 9:3-7)** This was a very stern and serious warning that God gave Solomon. God meant what He said and, as the king's sons turned away and served other gods, the atmosphere changed from a peaceful, prosperous kingdom to treachery and anarchy that was appalling.

We must understand that when God's presence is resisted and offended, God lifts His hand of protection and blessing also. Human society becomes "dry" from the lack of revelation, refreshing and blessing that comes from God Himself. The land spirals downward into a lawless chaos because people do not know God nor follow His commandments. In the case of ancient Israel, they went from a people who could claim "Immanuel" to recognizing that God's presence had departed from them, which was "Ichabod." They didn't value the presence of God enough to discipline themselves to protect it. **"On that day I will become angry with them and forsake them; I will hide my face and they will be destroyed. Many disasters and difficulties will come upon them, and on that day they will ask, 'Have not these disasters come upon us because God is not with us?'" (Deuteronomy 31:17-18)**

After many sequential warnings and tears shed by the prophets, God finally judged the widespread idolatry of His people. Jerusalem was conquered by Babylonian King Nebuchadnezzar in 597 A.D. Jewish survivors were taken captive and went into exile under the Babylonians. The dispersion of God's people lasted 70 years. Eventually, they were allowed to return to Jerusalem to rebuild the temple and re-activate their worship under the leadership of Ezra. But the restored temple did not compare to the former glory of the temple that Solomon built.

National repentance was a long road back for Ezra followed by Nehemiah. God gave specific correction through the prophet Malachi, advising the people how to win back the blessing of God's presence and regain the peace and prosperity they once knew. But the people found that it was much harder to regain what was lost than if they had simply obeyed and protected God's wonderful presence in the first place. We hear God answering the people's complaints and skepticism against Him in the Book of Malachi. Yet, in true redemptive form, God does not make repentance so unbearable that it would be overwhelming. God named certain offenses that He had against the people, but most of all He named the lack of integrity on the part of the priesthood as the main offense.

Through the prophet Malachi, God repeated what He heard the people saying. Disillusioned, they said that life was hard and God's presence and protection was minimal compared to the blessing that the nation once enjoyed. **"You also say, my, how tiresome it is! And you disdainfully sniff at it... and you bring what was taken by robbery, and what is lame or sick; so you bring that offering! Should I receive that from your hand? Says the Lord" (Malachi 1:13)** The people reminisced about the good old days, but God also remembered when His Spirit delighted in the heart-felt offerings made by the tribe of Levi as they carefully handled His presence. **"My covenant may continue with Levi, says the Lord of Hosts...so he revered Me and stood in awe of my Name...he walked with me in** peace and uprightness, and he turned many back from iniquity." (Malachi 2:4-6)

God longed for the days of old when the priests stood before Him in purity of heart. He told them that He would send His messenger who will come like a "refiner's fire," to display God's zeal for righteousness with a holy hatred of sin. Then the Lord carefully delineated the specific offenses that held back His presence. **"I will be a swift witness against the sorcerers and against the adulterers and against those who swear falsely..." (Malachi 3:5)**

Malachi Chapter 3 must be taken as a whole, not simply a chapter on how to restore finances. Often the real promise of this chapter is taken out of context making it sound as if God will cause money to "fall from the sky" if we pay our tithes. But this rendition is not at all what God is saying. Withholding the tithe was just one of the specific sins that was mentioned through Malachi.

The actual promise that God made to His people was a renewed outpouring of His Spirit and the felt grace of His presence that was lacking due to their sin and half-hearted worship, including their tithes. God was trying to remind the people of their former glory when Israel was a land of plenty due to the undeniable blessing of Immanuel.

The only hope that Israel, or any other people group or nation has is to repent, turn back to God and seek God's forgiveness. The hope lies in wooing God's presence, courting Him once again that He might return and heal the land. **"If I shut up the heavens so that there is no rain...And my people who are called by My name humble themselves and pray, and seek My face and turn from their wicked ways, then I will hear from heaven, will forgive their sin and will heal their land." (2 Chronicles 7:14)** God promises to hear and to heal us only if we corporately humble ourselves and seek God alone. We have to miss His presence enough to implore Him to return. Personal sanctification must accompany this kind of prayer. We have to take personal responsibility. Otherwise, we are just doing lip service because, in our hearts, we are standing in self-righteousness expecting everyone else to get right and repent. The more we point fingers, the worse the condition grows.

The real blessing that God wants to pour out is Himself. The Book of Malachi is actually a specific list of complaints that God had against His people that was holding back His presence from them. In the same way, we do not have to be ignorant about the specific sins in a church, area or nation that are offending God's Spirit. In His kindness towards us, God is willing that we repent. He will name the specific offenses to those who sincerely seek Him and are serious about getting things right.

God longs to open the heavens on our behalf, but He can't until we meet His conditions of true repentance. God will speak to people and reveal the specific offenses to those who have an ear to hear, keeping in mind that it is God's undeterred goal to be Immanuel.

Repentance is what we need in order to come back to friendship with God and value His presence as our most important possession. Man's primary problem is that he is bent on following his own predetermined thoughts, ideas and opinions rather than hear from God. **"This includes you who were once so far away from God. You were his enemies and hated Him and were separated from Him by your evil thoughts and actions, yet know he has brought you back as his friends." (Colossians 1:21)** The only path back to the presence and pleasure of God is to be broken of our stubborn mindsets that oppose His will and offend His presence. We have to fall out of love with what we think and have the humility to love and welcome His voice. **"Today if you hear His voice, do not harden your hearts, as when they provoked Me." (Hebrews 3:15)**

The Lord promised to send a messenger who would come in the power of Elijah in order to make things right and cleanse the land of sin. Malachi was the last prophetic voice who was heard until the time of John the Baptist 400 years later. Let's go on to see how John the Baptist fulfilled God's requirement of repentance and was able to single-handedly restore the priesthood to a manner that was pleasing enough to bless the land with an outpouring of His presence.

.

CHAPTER SIX

❦

MINISTERING TO THE LORD

J ohn the Baptist was the messenger that Malachi pro-phetically spoke of who would make a way for the return of God's presence as in the former glory. In fact, the glory of God's presence would be even greater. Both of John's parents were descendants of the tribe of Levi. His father Zacharias was of the division of Abijah and his mother Elizabeth a direct descendant of Aaron. Zacharias min-istered regularly at the temple and they were both found pleasing and righteous in God's sight due to their rever-ence and obedience. **"And they were both righteous in the sight of God, walking blamelessly in all the command-ments and requirements of the Lord." (Luke 1:6)**

One day as Zacharias was offering incense inside of the temple, an angel appeared to him and told him that Elizabeth would conceive and their son John would be the forerunner of the Christ. **"And it is he who will go as a forerunner before Him in the spirit and power of Elijah, to turn the hearts of the fathers back to the children and the disobedient to the attitude of righteousness; so as to make ready a people prepared for the Lord." (Luke 1:17)** The ministry of John was one of revealing sin to people so that they would repent and return to God. Again, we see God's longstanding pledge to have a holy people for

Himself so that He could dwell among them now as God in the flesh.

At this time, God was not satisfied with the half-hearted perfunctory ministry of the priests at the temple. They were simply going through the motions of religious rituals that had no real effect on the hearts of the people. Their actions were according to the Law, but they had departed from the highest law which was to love the Lord with all their heart, mind, soul and strength.

Under the anointing of the Holy Spirit, John lived in the desert region until his time of ministry to Israel. This was to fulfill the prophecy of Isaiah foretelling one who would cry out from the wilderness. **"A voice is calling, 'Clear the way for the Lord in the wilderness; make smooth in the desert a highway for our God.'" (Isaiah 40:3)** Under the direction of the Holy Spirit, John became the type of priest that God was really looking for, ministering to Him in true heartfelt repentance for the sins of the people. The sacrifice of a broken and contrite heart was actually what God wanted. John's humility effectively ministered to the Lord.

Because of right ministry, John was able to clear the spiritual barriers to create an atmosphere that was conducive for the Holy Spirit. The springs of God's presence poured forth in the desert, just like the prophet Isaiah had foretold. **"Behold I will do something new, now it will spring forth...I will even make a roadway in the wilderness, rivers in the desert...Because I have given waters in the wilderness and rivers in the desert to give drink to my chosen people." (Isaiah 43:19-20)** John's ministry made it possible for the Son of God, Jesus, to step into His public ministry. At that time, John was baptizing the people in the River Jordan for the forgiveness of their sins. Jesus underwent John's baptism of repentance even though He was sinless. By doing so, Christ fulfilled the repentance of Israel that God had been calling for through the Old Testament prophets.

God accepted Christ's identification repentance as the heavens opened and the Holy Spirit filled the area with God's presence. **"Now it came about when all the people were baptized, that Jesus also was baptized, and while He was praying, heaven was opened, and the Holy Spirit descended upon Him in bodily form like a dove…"** (Luke 3:21-22) This was the blessing of an open heaven that had been promised through Malachi. God endorsed the work of His Son by a voice from Heaven that everyone heard. **"…And a voice came out of Heaven, 'Thou are My beloved Son, in Thee I am well pleased.'"** (Luke 3:22)

With Jesus, the tabernacle was no longer a place, but rather a Person. He was the perfect "meeting place" where God meets man in one Person. He was God incarnate who had taken on the "tent" of human flesh. So the temple of worship was, is and will always be Christ Himself. We not only worship Christ, but we also worship *in* Christ. Christ successfully ushered in the presence of God, just like the tent of meeting of Moses and the temple of Solomon. Christ became the bridge to restored relationship and co-habitation with man that God always intended. He is the approved way for man to come into the holy presence of God.

Christians today have the privilege and the responsibility to stand before God and minister to Him just like John the Baptist and the Levites once did. This is referred to in the Bible as "the priesthood of all believers." To ensure that there would always be a faithful priesthood ministering to the Lord, God opened up the priesthood to all who believe. People no longer have to be descendents of the house of Levi.

Again, this act shows the undeterred commitment of God to have a holy people close to Him who value His presence enough to worship Him freely and look after His relational needs. **"That they may minister to Me." (Exodus 28:1)** The invitation to minister before the Lord with sacrifices of praise and thanksgiving is given to "whomever." **"I will look with favor on the faithful of the land, so that they may live with me; whoever walks in the way that is blameless shall minister to Me." (Psalm 101:6)**

The priesthood that God established through Aaron and his sons became a ministry to continue for all generations. **"Their anointing shall qualify them for a perpetual priesthood throughout their generations." (Exodus 40:15)** This fulfills God's Word to have a kingdom of priests on earth to mirror the myriads of holy angels who worship and minister to God in heaven. **"...and He has made us to be a kingdom, priests to His God and Father..." (Revelation 1:6)**

Instead of Aaron, we now have Jesus who became our High Priest. He not only intercedes on our behalf, but also allows us to participate in this same privileged ministry on behalf of others. **"For it was fitting that we should have such a high priest, holy, blameless, undefiled, separated from sinners, and exalted above the heavens. Unlike the other high priests, he has no need to offer sacrifices day after day, first for his own sins, and then for those of the people." (Hebrews 7:26-27)**

The sacrifices that we now offer are simply sacrifices of praise, thanksgiving, worship and right confession to minister to God correctly. **"...you also, as living stones, are being built up as a spiritual house for a holy priesthood, to offer us spiritual sacrifices acceptable to God through Jesus Christ." (1 Peter 2:5)** The altar upon which we offer these spiritual sacrifices is our new life in Christ where we slay the flesh of the old life through obedience. **"I urge you therefore brethren, by the mercies of God, to present your bodies a living and holy sacrifice, accept-**

able to God which is your spiritual service of worship." (Romans 12:1) God has always been more interested in matters of the human heart, not in the sacrifice of bulls and goats. This is our time to express our love and appreciation through prayer to our wonderful God who enjoys hearing our voice going out to Him. He delights when we call out to Him. This exchange is what He always had in mind since the beginning of time.

The exciting principle about this new order of priests is that Christ is positioned in heavenly places as our High Priest and we also minister from there. The Bible says that, as believers and followers of Christ, we are now seated in heavenly places with Him. "...even when we were dead in our transgressions, made us alive together with Christ...and raised us up with Him, and seated us with Him in the heavenly places; in Christ Jesus, in order that in the ages to come He might show the surpassing riches of His grace in kindness toward us in Christ Jesus." (Ephesians 2:5-7) This is a matter of position that has been won for us. Every believer now sits side-by-side with Christ. Jesus won back the original position that was lost by Adam, the place next to God as His suitable companion and personal priest. We have to realize what a strategic opportunity this is for us. This makes our prayers and supplications immensely powerful because we offer them in the very throne room of God!

The reason why we need to get out of sin and self-righteousness is because those mindsets tell us that we are not worthy or that we must earn this position by doing something first. Our place as priests next to Jesus has been established, bequeathed and revealed to us. Again, the works of God are this: simply believe and obey. This place with Christ gives us a tremendous vantage point because it takes us higher and into deeper into relationship with Him. From here, God can reveal the secrets of His kingdom.

As priests who are seated in heavenly places, we can do much that has eternal consequence. When the priesthood is intact, the priests can minister to the Lord by welcoming and honoring His presence. We can offer up worship as sacrifices that are pleasing to God. The worship of the priests offset the resistance of carnal man who holds God's presence in contempt. They act as a buffer zone to protect the presence of God from the hard-hearted resistance of "climbers" who have answered the call of Babylon to serve self. They want nothing to do with the presence of God because of the direction that they have chosen to take. **"And this is the judgment, that the light is come into the world, and men loved the darkness rather than the light, for their deeds were evil." (John 3:19)**

Fortunately, God is patient, not wanting any to perish in their evil deeds, but wanting all men to come to repentance. Therefore, God's heart is soothed by the petitions and ministry of the righteous buffer zone of priests, who minister blessings to Him and extend His grace, mercy and kindness to people on His behalf.

Jesus said that God the Father is seeking those who will worship Him in spirit and in truth. **"But an hour is coming, and now is, when the true worshipers shall worship the Father in spirit and truth; for such people the Father seeks to be His worshipers." (John 4:23)** Jesus said this to the Samaritan woman that He met at the well when she questioned Him about the place of worship for her people. His conversation with the woman verifies God's sincere desire to accept whoever will worship Him with a right heart and according to what He says in the Bible. God is looking for consecrated worshipers who will woo His presence and beckon Him to come and abide with them.

Like King David, we must develop a hunger for the presence of God and value the importance of having

Immanuel. David knew from his intimate worship that God's desire was to have a resting place, a habitation where His presence would be comfortable to come and remain. **"For the Lord has chosen Zion; he has desired it for his habitation; this is my resting place forever; here I will reside, for I have desired it." (Psalm 132:13)** Following in the footsteps of David, worshipers transcend from religious rigor to relational preference. We go from duty to desire, from "have to" to "want to." We train ourselves in the nuances of God in order to relate well to a God who is holy and who is Spirit.

Only in the context of a carefully developed friendship does God begin to bare Himself to disclose His relational needs. Although we know Him as a Rock and a Fortress, we start to know the softer side of His personality. We see that He is a God who needs to be needed and wants to be wanted. We are His wife who listens intently to the strong voice of her husband. When he lowers his voice, she knows that he is about to tell her his heart. This is the heart-to-heart place that Christ has attained for us in order to hear our Kingly Lover speak. Like taking a pulse in the life of a marriage, we lean in and see if there are any offenses that may interrupt the seamlessness of oneness. He may also give you a heart-warming compliment to show you that He hears.

God is certainly there for us to be strong and mighty whenever we need Him. There is no lack of power in Him and no weakness in His character. But as we mature in Christ, we stretch ourselves to find out more about God's relational qualities. We must avail ourselves to meet His need to bare His eternal soul. This is the close friendship that God had with Moses and with many others. He longs to also have this kind of friendship with "whomever."

Let me give some practical steps on developing this kind of relationship. The Bible says that we are to come into the presence of God with praise and thanksgiving. **"Enter His gates with thanksgiving, and His courts with praise; Give thanks to Him; bless His name." (Psalm 100:4)** This is vital to approaching God correctly. Meeting with God does not depend upon what you do, but upon who He is. He is highly relational and loves to interact with us. Christ became the meeting place, the tabernacle, so that we could have simple access to God. He will respond to us when we quiet ourselves and seek to come into His presence. We can play some worship music if that is available or just sit with a Bible open and give Him some time to speak.

During our time of tabernacle, we can exercise our priestly privilege by ministering to the Lord. Discipline yourself to put your needs and requests on "the back burner" for a short time. Come before God in an attitude of adoration and love. This is the time for you to express your desire for Him alone. Tell Him how much your want Him and need Him. Thank Him for revealing Himself to you and that you want to know Him more. Dive into the flood of His presence with words that are directed to Him and about Him. The Holy Spirit will help you by teaching you how to worship as Heaven worships! Enjoy giving God pleasure. Know that what you are doing is right and good, fully aligned with the on-going worship in Heaven. Invite Him to share Himself with you. Ask for the fullness of His presence to envelop you. Minister to Him to shield His Spirit from the daily rejection of unrepentant man. Let Him know that He is welcome, received and sought after. **"Bless the Lord, all you His hosts, you who serve Him by doing His will. Bless the Lord, all you works of His, in all places of His dominion; Bless the Lord, O my soul!" (Psalm 103:21-22)**

After some time, the Holy Spirit will come to with you. As a Christian, the Holy Spirit is already inside of you, giving you this desire and knowledge of how to meet with God. He is also upon you and will work in the atmosphere that surrounds you to make you aware of His eternal presence. The room atmosphere may change to become lighter and brighter. There may be a sense of peace and joy that replaces tension and gloom. You will begin to feel His warmth and His love will surround you.

At this point, do what the Holy Spirit directs you to do. If He gives you insight to turn to a specific passage in Scripture, then do so. Read it to yourself or, even better, read it out loud. Read line by line so that the Holy Spirit can give you what God wants to say. He will explain things to you in a biblical context using spiritual language. This is not a complicated experience. Just sit and receive from Him the insight that He wants you to have. One sentence from God's Word has the supernatural ability to instantly resolve the most complicated human problems and let you know that He cares.

You may start to weep in the presence of God as He personally touches you. This is very real and very normal. God can release us from heavy burdens that we were not aware of. **"Casting all your anxiety upon Him, because He cares for you..." (1 Peter 5:7)** Go ahead and cry if He touches you deeply. We sometimes need emotional release and may not even know it. He knows our inner most needs. He is a Teacher but also a Healer. This meeting with God is not about more knowledge but about more of Him. **"In my distress, I called upon the Lord, and cried to my God for help; He heard my voice out of His temple, and my cry for help before Him came to His ears." (Psalm 18:6)** God's presence may come over you in such a strong way that it grips you and you feel that you cannot move. This is powerful and good! Don't resist Him by letting your mind wander or think that you are too busy to wait in His presence. We need to allow the presence of God to have

His pleasure of spending time with us. This is the abiding tabernacle experience that we were made for.

On a side note, our time with God's holy presence is not a mystical "trance" as in Yoga or Transcendental Meditation. We do not have to recite a mantra or the Name of God over and over in order to summons Him. Nor do we want to get into some hypnotic state through vain repetition as we try to blank our mind out. We also do not want to get into a habit of trying to "visualize" Jesus. Those practices are all forms of "channeling" where people go out under the power of demonic spirits and lose their conscious awareness. In prayer, our mind is active and engaged. If need be, we could pull ourselves away in order to answer a phone call because we would hear it ringing. But if we value the presence of God, we would not interrupt what God is doing.

Another issue that comes up is the objection, "How will I find the time to do this?" My suggestion is to re-align your activities and show your love for God by guarding your time. Don't waste hours of precious time watching nonsensical shows on television. Cut back your time on the internet and monitor your communication on electronic devices. You have to set your own schedule to have time to meet with God. This is communication with Heaven that counts. Don't pass up the chance to be His faithful priest.

In our tabernacle meeting with God, He may speak to us about some specific sin that offends Him. He may give us a vivid picture what we are doing, cutting through our reasons and excuses. This is the conviction power of the Holy Spirit doing His work of sanctification. We should welcome His correction and chose to repent and forsake the activity or attitude that He is pointing to.

Another important aspect of tabernacle is that God will supply power and give us inner strength as He fills us with His Spirit. **"And do not get drunk with wine, for that** is dissipation, but be filled with the Spirit." (Ephesians 5:18) As God fills our inner being with His Spirit, we will have the courage to go forward with a real sense of His backing. We must take time to develop our spiritual senses to know what God "feels" like. Jesus complained to the religious leaders that they did not know the scriptures nor the power of God. They were filled with head knowledge through memorization, but they did not sense His presence and His power in order to submit themselves to it.

One of the most important aspects of coming into the presence of God is to be able to understand His purposes upon the earth above our own. Simply put, God's holiness forms the back drop for people to be able to recognize His mercy. We fall in love with Him when we realize how unmerited His grace is. God's wants to be most known for His holiness, but He is glorified and celebrated for His mercy. **"O Lord, I have heard of your renown, and I stand in awe, O Lord, of your work. In our own time revive it; in our own time make it known, in wrath may you remember your mercy." (Habakkuk 3:1-2)**

God's desire to preserve human life now and forevermore is His most dominant purpose upon the earth. He did not create us to die, but to live. **"Have I any pleasure in the death of the wicked, says the Lord God, and not rather that they should turn from their ways and live?" (Ezekiel 18:23)** God's purposes on earth involve strategies for human redemption, to preserve life and enable people to have a restored relationship with Himself. God is waiting for people to turn to Him and cry out for His mercy. He is willing to send help from Heaven when people get over their self-righteousness and self-satisfaction to acknowledge their utter need of Him. **"Therefore the Lord longs to be gracious to you, and therefore He waits on high to have compassion on you. For the Lord is a God of justice; How blessed are those who long for Him...He**

**will surely be gracious to you at the sound of your cry;
When He hears it He will answer you." (Isaiah 30:18-19)**
Ask for His mercy to touch people and situations that you
are aware of.

In keeping with His purposes of preserving human life
and order upon the earth, God says that He will give us
strategies to participate in. Part of the tabernacle experience is receiving the vision of His plans that we can be
vitally a part of. We can be involved through prayer to
make His name known and offer the good news of Jesus
Christ to those who need the Savior. Our position in the
heavenlies as Christians gives us the perfect vantage point
to make our priestly appeal to God and bless people
through intercession.

With this in mind, let's continue on to see what it
means to "stand in the gap" for the sake of others.

CHAPTER SEVEN

❧

STANDING IN THE GAP

God wants the grace of His presence to rule the earth rather than the power of sin and death. Since He has revealed this as His will, then we can believe that He has the power and integrity to do what He says. **"And the Law came in that the transgression might increase; but where sin increased, grace abounded all the more, that, as sin reigned in death, even so grace might reign through righteousness to eternal life through Jesus Christ our Lord."** **(Romans 5:20-21)** When sin rules people's lives, it triumphs in a negative way through permanent separation from God. But God has made it possible for sin not to be the "winner," but instead the "loser." Through the forgiveness of sin that Christ obtained, people can have the unmerited pardon that God supplied.

There is earth-shaking power in the forgiveness of God through Jesus Christ. The moment that Jesus gave up His life for the forgiveness of sin, the Bible cites, **"And behold, the veil of the temple was torn in two from the top to bottom, and the earth shook; the rocks were split, and the tombs were opened; and many bodies of the saints who had fallen asleep were raised..."** **(Matthew 27:51-52)** People were raised from the grave and came alive again— were revived—when Christ forgave sin. When Jesus cried out for our forgiveness from the Cross, He successfully broke the power of sin and death. The ground trembled and boulders were shattered when divine forgiveness was unleashed. The domain of darkness felt the tremors of defeat. It was the beginning of the end for Satan. Please remember that the forgiveness of God is intensely powerful.

This is why God is looking for people to understand their position as priests who can come before Him and stand in the gap. The fruit of intercession is to seek God's mercy and forgiveness, bring God's conviction power, proclaim healing and usher in revival. Those who minister to the Lord can ask Him to forgive specific offenses and pray for God's will to occur. Can we possibly grasp the effects that we can have when we fulfill our priestly vocation?

We can ask God to supply His grace so that His presence will abound and exercise its dominion rather than sin. Repentance ministry is about preparing the spiritual atmosphere to make a habitation for the presence of God. Revival does not happen without repentance of sin. People must become aware of their transgressions against a holy God and be willing to forsake sin and turn to God on His terms.

In their book *Rivers of Revival*, Neil T. Anderson and Elmer L. Towns cite repentance as an absolute key to revival for an area. In their chapter on repentance, they explain, "The people of God must repent and turn away from their sin to serve the true living God. Without repentance, people cannot enjoy fellowship with God."[40]

God's harsh judgment only comes by default after His offer of grace is refused and exhausted. There is an end to God's patience, but we do not know the extent of that grace and it is probably more far reaching than we could

---

40 *Rivers of Revival*, P. 160

ever imagine. As God's holy priesthood, we must stay on the side of mercy and grace, stay out of self-righteous judgment and seek God for His kindness that leads people to repentance. **"Behold then the kindness and severity of God; to those who fell, severity, but to you, God's kindness...if you continue in His kindness, otherwise you also will be cut off." (Romans 11:22)** This is an encouragement to us but also a warning that our intercession is to always want the best for people, asking for God's mercy to come rather than His harsh judgment. We did nothing to deserve His kindness and so we want to extend that same generosity through prayer for others.

God is looking for His followers to stand before Him in prayer and ask for grace and goodness for others. He longs to have sanctified believers who will come to Him and seek forgiveness on behalf of sinners. Those who mature in the sanctification process have tremendous sway with God, just as in the examples of Abraham and Moses. **"Who shall ascend the hill of the Lord? And who shall stand in his holy place: Those who have clean hands and pure hearts, who do not lift up their soul to what is false and do not swear deceitfully. They will receive a blessing from the Lord..." (Psalm 24:3-4)** These types of saints bridge the distance between the sinner and God by strategically "standing in the gap." Let me explain why.

There are two activities that go on day and night before the throne of God. The first is legalistic accusing by Satan. **"For the accuser of our comrades has been thrown down, who accuses them day and night before our God." (Revelation 12:10)** This activity is done by mentioning specific sins that people are involved with, reminding God of His wrath against sin and pressing for harsh judgment upon people, cities or nations. Satan hates us and wants the worst for us. God has revealed that this activity is going on, although we are not fully aware of it.

But because we have been told about it, we must rally to bring our "counter-claim" of intercession.

Hear the emotions of God through this scripture as He searches for those who can stand before Him to intercede to dissuade Him from harsh judgment. **"No one calls for justice; no one pleads his case with integrity..." (Isaiah 59:4)** This highlights the value of being a Christian with integrity, who can call out for justice without hypocrisy. God is displeased when He finds no one who will go before Him in prayer to plead for Him to stop injustice. He wants us to be moved enough to want to move Him! **"The Lord looked and was displeased that there was no justice. He saw that there was none, he was appalled that there was no one to intervene." (Isaiah 59:15-16)**

In his book *The Power of One Christlike Life*, Francis Frangipane makes this rousing comment about the power of holiness combined with intercession. "As much as they are moved with compassion for the lost, their primary quest is not to touch their neighbors' hearts, but to touch the heart of God. They know if they awaken the Father's pleasure, the power of the Spirit will go before them. God Himself will change the hearts around them."[41] I have presented in this book that God is committed to come and invade our world with His presence, but this author uses the word "obsessed." I like his version better!

The Church is called to a degree of holiness to be God's suitable companion so that we can administer grace, which is our priestly duty. If we, who are seated in the heavenlies with Christ, pursue God to forgive and relent from harsh judgment, He has shown in biblical history that He will do so. Showing mercy is actually God's first choice in dealing with people. **"And I sought for anyone among them who would repair the wall and stand in the breach before me**

---

41 *The Power of One Christlike Life*, P. 16

on behalf of the land so that I would not destroy it..." **(Ezekiel 22:30)** God is looking for righteous intercessors to hear His heart and His complaints against an area or city and then go before Him to ask for mercy. In the Book of Amos, God showed the prophet the destruction that He had planned for the city and the prophet cried out to God. As a result, the Lord relented from His plans, to His glory. Such weighty say-so in human matters is hard to comprehend. But that is exactly the position of authority that was at one time held by Adam and Eve. God can now duplicate the same human jurisdiction through those who meet with Him and hear Him out. Scripture names at least five men, Noah, Moses, Samuel, Daniel and Job, who had a level of favor with God that they could stand before God, stretch themselves out over the sins of the people, and turn back God's judgment from the land.

The strategy of "identification repentance" is given to us through the example of Jesus who, through John's baptism, repented on behalf of Israel. When God names specific sins, just as at the time of Malachi, repentance ministers can go before God and apologize on behalf of others. We can minister to God's heart through sincere "I am sorry" confessions. God accepted Jesus' repentance as a substitute for those who wouldn't repent for themselves. We can stand in the gap to offer substitute apologies that God will accept in order to cleanse the land.

Another example from scripture is the identification repentance by the prophet Daniel. **"While I was speaking, and was praying and confessing my sin and the sin of my people Israel..." (Daniel 9:20)** Daniel confessed for himself and also his people, even though he was not directly involved in the rebellion and idolatry that they had displayed. He knew about what they had done and he confessed what he knew. In the New Testament, the Apostle Paul was the man chosen by God to stand in the gap on behalf of the Gentiles. **"Nevertheless on some points I have written to you rather boldly by way of reminder, because of the grace given to me by God to be a minister of Christ Jesus to the Gentiles in the priestly service of the gospel of God, so that the offering of the Gentiles may be acceptable, sanctified by the Holy Spirit." (Romans 15:15)** Both of these godly men made an appeal to God based on His mercy that He would grant the grace for people to turn back to God.

Probably one of the most stunning displays of humility and repentance was the woman Abigail in the Old Testament. She feared God and knew God's purposes for David's life as the future king of Israel. Unfortunately, she was married to a selfish, unspiritual brute named Nabal, which means "fool." Nabal resisted God's purposes by refusing to feed David's men after a military campaign that protected Nabal's livestock. This man's ingratitude so angered David that he went to kill Nabal.

When Abigail found out about the coming judgment, she immediately fixed the provisions that David needed and personally rushed to the scene to offer what David had requested. She bowed before David and told him that her husband's actions were all her fault—that she was totally to blame. She bowed low before him and begged him for a pardon. (1 Samuel 25: 23-28) David was stunned by her actions and he relented. She successfully talked David out of harsh judgment that he had planned, reminding him of his calling as a merciful king. This woman so endeared David that, when he heard that Nabal died, he sent for Abigail to marry her.

We glean a strategy in intercession from this story called "repentance, worship and warfare." The repentant intercessor, Abigail, marries David who is king of worship and king of warfare. United together through corporate prayer, this three-stranded cord can be applied as an effective weapon in our prayer arsenal. We can employ these elements as we minister to the Lord.

Just like Abigail, we can enjoy intimacy with God like a wife who He confides in. We can get to know God's heart and appeal to Him to pour out His grace. He will entrust us with higher strategies as we listen to how He speaks. This kind of diligent listening creates the place of tabernacle where His presence abides. **"And where is a place that I may rest? For my hands made all these things, thus they came into being; declares the Lord, But to this one I will look, to him who is humble and contrite in spirit, and who trembles at my word." (Isaiah 66:2)**

In this place of tabernacle God will hear and exert power to preserve life. **"God does not take away life; instead, he devises ways so that a banished person may not remain estranged from him." (2 Samuel 14:14)** From this verse, we can hear God's heart to extend His grace to those who are far away from Him. We must mature in our attitudes toward God and to seek His higher purposes.

"Come up here, and I will show you what must take place." (Revelation 4:1-2) Through our relationship with Him, we can bring in life-saving help by operating from our higher vantage point. He will listen to those who boldly go before Him and ask for grace and mercy in time of need. Through diligent repentance, we can have times of refreshing from the movement of the Holy Spirit. **"Repent, therefore, and turn to God so that your sins may be wiped out, so that times of refreshing may come from the presence of the Lord..." (Acts 3:19)** If we learn to value and protect the presence of God, then His presence will be poured out to bring refreshing to a dry and weary land.

CHAPTER EIGHT

✑

TABERNACLE

After the repentance ministry of Elijah in the Old Testament, God began to heal and water the land through the ministry and miracles of Elisha. God began to restore the barren dry places. Where there had been death, He brought forth life. The first miracle of Elisha was to heal the water in the city of Jericho. After receiving a report about the bad water in the city that could not support life, Elisha took a new bowl with salt in it and threw the salt into the spring. **"This is what the Lord says: I have healed this water. Never again will it cause death or make the land unproductive.' And the water has remained wholesome to this day according to the work Elisha had spoken."** (2 Kings 2:21-22)

In another instance, Elisha filled a whole valley with water. This was to counter and restore the land after the word that Elijah had spoken to bring three years of no rain. Now, because of the repentance ministry of Elijah, God forgave sin and began to heal the land. In fact, God said it was an easy thing for Him and something that He wants to do. **"This is what the Lord says: Make this valley full of ditches. For this is what the Lord says: You will see neither wind nor rain, yet this valley will be filled with water, and you, your cattle and your other animals will** drink. **This is an easy thing in the eyes of the Lord...the next morning, about the time for offering the sacrifice, there it was—water flowing from the direction of Edom! And the land was filled with water."** **(2 Kings 3:16-20)** God has plans to heal and restore our families, our cities and our land if we will only turn to Him, repent and welcome His presence as our vital answer.

There are many promises of restoration that God says He will supply of we will humble ourselves and meet His conditions. We have to look for promises that start with "If..." and see the list of conditions in order to obtain the promised "then..." For example, **"If you follow my statutes and keep my commandments and observe them faithfully** (then) **I will give you rains in their season and the land shall yield its produce." (Deuteronomy 28:9-12)** We cannot take it upon ourselves to skip over the conditions and then expect to obtain the restorative promises. We must obediently meet God's conditions and believe that He will fulfill His Word.

Another example is from the Book of Joel. It says that if we return to God with all of our hearts, with fasting and weeping, rend our hearts before Him, gather the elders and call a solemn assembly for corporate repentance, then God says that He will pour out His Spirit upon all mankind. **"And it will come about after this that I will pour out My Spirit on all mankind..." (Joel 2:28)** Once again, we can see the blessing that extends beyond the Church when we minister to Him. This outpouring of His Spirit is how people will know that He is in our midst and that there is no other God on earth besides Him.

God promises us that the latter splendor of His tabernacle will be even greater than the first. Those who pursue their relationship with Jesus will have a growing sense of His presence. Corporately, we can have a greater measure of Immanuel when we welcome His presence and minister to Him through corporate worship and prayer. **"The latter splendor of this house shall be greater than the former, says the Lord of Hosts; and in this place I will give prosperity, says the Lord of Hosts."** (Haggai 2:9) How much greater will the glory and beauty of Christ Himself exceed the glory of the temple of Solomon which was exceptionally beautiful in its day. Christ's glory is beyond comprehension. **"O Lord, I love the house in which you dwell, and the place where your glory abides."** (Psalm 26:8) Do we love the place where God dwells? Isn't that what we want?

Tabernacle. This is where we will dwell with God forever. If we love His presence now, we certainly will be saturated by His presence in Heaven. He will fill us completely and we will never feel the weakness and empty void that sin caused ever again. We will live in an indescribable euphoria as we are surrounded by His love. **"One thing I have asked from the Lord, that I shall seek; that I may dwell in the house of the Lord all the days of my life, to behold the beauty of the Lord, and to meditate in His temple."** (Psalm 27:4-6)

Someday as His followers, we will see the full journey that we have taken by faith. We will see the long road and why He chose to send us the way He did. It will all make perfect sense and we will be glad for the maturity that we gained from all the lessons along the way. **"God hath saved us, and called us with a holy calling, not according to our own works, but according to His own purpose and grace, which was given us in Christ Jesus."** (2 Timothy 1:8-9) Someday we will see how we glorified God.

In this world, "climbers" who answered the call of Babylon will have their portion of whatever material gain that they have gathered for themselves. But they will be sadly empty-handed in eternity. But for the Levites who have made the personal vow, "the Lord is my portion," they will be the richest people in Heaven because they have chosen the most valuable commodity, who is Christ Jesus.

There will be a segment of people who will have the closest proximity to the King who sits on the throne. These will be those who suffered for the sake of the kingdom and worshiped God with their lives, even unto death. But they are also the ones who chose to die to sin and self in order to give themselves fully to God. These are the priests that will have their portion forever! **"These are they who have come out of the great ordeal; they have washed their robes and made them white in the blood of the Lamb. For this reason they are before the throne of God and worship Him day and night within His temple, and the one who is seated on the throne will shelter them." (Revelation 7:13-15)**

God's rewards for righteousness will be felt in eternity. But even now, we can have His peace, prosperity, protection and good health because of His presence with us. He says that His rewards are with Him. **"Behold, the Lord God will come with might, with His arm ruling for Him. Behold His reward is with Him and His recompense before Him." (Isaiah 40:10)**

God says that He will bring healing and recovery if we repent and work to restore the relationship that He once had at the time of the tabernacle. He also says that He will return our prosperity if we repent and minister to Him. **"I am going to bring recovery and healing, I will heal them and reveal to them abundance of prosperity and security. I will restore the fortunes of Israel and rebuild them as they were at first." (Jeremiah 33:6-9)**

God also promises the excitement of allowing us to know the secrets of the kingdom. He wants to teach us His amazing ways and give us spiritual insight that will impress us with His love and goodness. **"He answered, 'To**

you it has been given to know the secrets of the kingdom of heaven.'" (Matthew 13:11-12) These secrets are not just to know more but to know and appreciate Jesus more.

Man's accomplishments will not be celebrated in eternity. Only God's His accomplishments will be recognized and celebrated. This is why we must learn to become famous with God rather than famous with man, because earthly fame is short-lived and gone forever. **"Not to us, O Lord, not to us, but to your name be glory." (Psalm 115:1)**

From the outside, the tabernacle of Moses looked drab and unattractive to the onlooker. There was nothing to make man desire it. The desire had to come from within to want to know God and want to be with God. Jesus told two parables that summarize the attitude that we need to have for God's presence. They represent a hidden treasure that, once discovered, is worth selling everything in order to possess it. **"The kingdom of heaven is like a treasure hidden in the field, which a man found and hid; and from joy over it he goes and sells all that he has, and buys that field. Again the kingdom of heaven is like a merchant seeking fine pearls, and upon finding one pearl of great value, he went and sold all that he had, and bought it." (Matthew 13:44-46)** The one thing that makes the kingdom so valuable is that it is the dwelling place for the King. Jesus Christ is truly the pearl of great price. Our desire should be the excitement, thrill and pleasure of having Him now and forever. One day we will see past the drab covering that hides this treasure as His radiant majesty is unveiled for all to see.

There will be a circle of priests surrounding His throne because that is His prescribed way to protect His holy presence. That ring of priests will be the royal priesthood of the men and women who learned to value His presence while on earth. There will no longer be a heavenly temple at the consummation of the marriage between man and God. Christ will open the heavenly temple and become the Tabernacle where man and God meet and dwell. Heaven's eternal activities will be bathed in worship and fellowship. Man's heart, still bearing the remembrance of the curse of sin, will no longer be divided by other loves. Nor will he dwell emotionally far off. Our hearts will be united and focused on Him just as our bodies will be united with Him; man and God dwelling together in naked, unashamed love. **"And I saw no temple in it, for the Lord God, the Almighty, and the Lamb, are its temple."** (Revelation 21:22) **"And I heard a loud voice from the throne saying, 'Behold, the tabernacle of God is among men, and He shall dwell among them and they shall be His people, and God Himself shall be among them…"** (Revelation 21:3)

Until then, we need to allow His fire to consume us until there is no more of us but only Him. This is the sacrifice that God loves to "smell" and fill His nostrils with like sweet incense. It is the scent of obedience and the fire of fierce trust. It is the odor of burning off human reasoning that opposes God's Word and purposely retraining our mind to simply believe. It is when we live in this daily fire that God responds by bringing His fire that shields and protects the precious daily sacrifice. For Him alone we keep the fire alive on the altar of our hearts with a deep desire to meet and abide in Christ.

Let's finish with a story from the Book of Daniel. Due to their idolatry and offense to the presence of God, God lifted His hand of protection from the Israelites. They were plundered and carried into exile by the forces of Nebuchadnezzar, the king of Babylon. Among the exiles were three youths from Jewish royal lineage who were chosen to be part of the king's court and were trained in the culture, wisdom and practices of the Chaldeans. This probably included the study of Astrology and other forms of divination. The three sons of Judah were re-named and give names of Chaldean gods: Shadrach, Meshach and Abednego.

The king of Babylon had erected a golden statue in the desert in his own honor and required the Babylonians to bow down and worship the image in tribute to himself. This again represents the ultimate goal of "climbers" to be seen and worshiped by other men. Despite that decree, the three Hebrew youths refused to worship the idolatrous image. They had come from a culture that was founded upon the worship of the Living God and, even though they were immersed in pagan culture, they chose to exclusively worship and serve Immanuel. The stories that they grew up listening to about the Pillar of Cloud by day and the Pillar of Fire by night were still vivid in their minds. If God could preserve their heritage nation Israel in the desert, then He could protect and preserve them now.

Nebuchadnezzar was enraged that the young men defied his orders. He acted upon his decree that anyone who would not worship the golden image would be thrown alive into a fiery furnace. **"But whoever does not fall down and worship shall immediately be cast into the midst of the furnace of blazing fire." (Daniel 3:6)** The young men were brought before the king to be destroyed as the furnace was heated up seven times hotter than normal to reflect the rage of the king.

As the Hebrew youths considered the consequences of their faith, they looked at each other with unwavering resolve. How could they now betray the love and faithfulness of the God of Israel that, at one time, had been the beacon of their nation? Would they follow in the sins of their forsaken people by practicing more idolatry? Or would they dare to take a stand to show their commitment to Yahweh? They staked their lives that the living God would regard them. But if He didn't, it wouldn't matter because they chose to pledge themselves in faithfulness to Him! They decided to simply trust.

As the fire in the furnace grew even more intense, their fears were strangely calmed. They were no longer aware of the caustic anger of the outraged king, but sensed a sweet peace and presence filling the arena. The three young men joined together as their boldness blazed even hotter than the fire that was prepared for them. This was the testimony that the young men gave that Babylonian king: **"If it be so, our God whom we serve is able to deliver us from the furnace of blazing fire; and he will deliver us out of your hand O King. But even if He does not, let it be know to you, O King, that we are not going to serve your gods or worship the golden image that you have set up." (Daniel 3:17-18)**

God heeded the cry and right confession of those three Hebrew youths. He saw their refusal to answer the call of Babylon to worship man-made gods. The youths were separate, consecrated in their hearts to the God that they knew and loved. In spite of pending danger, God saw "nuwach" buoyant in the hearts of those young men as they quietly rested and trusted in their God. Immanuel was there on the scene providing those Hebrew youths the power to make such a faith-filled claim. God's presence with them gave them the abiding peace, trust and faith that they displayed. They knew that He would be there for them because His presence was with them.

The fire from the furnace was intensely hot and consumed the soldiers who carried Shadrach, Meshach and Abednego who were bound with ropes and could not move. The king watched as the three youths were cast into the fire. Suddenly, the king saw an astounding sight as he came near to the door of the furnace. He saw four men unbound, walking around in the furnace and the fourth man had the appearance of a God! When the youths came out, their bodies and clothes were not burnt or even singed and they had no smell of smoke upon them!

How was this possible? From God's perspective, like the ark of Noah, the tent of meeting of Moses and the temple of Solomon, the fiery furnace in the midst of Babylon invited the presence of God and served as the perfect place for God to tabernacle with His followers. Before the eyes of an incredulous king, God and man co-existed in that blaze! God was pent up with His loyal children who loved Him enough to die for Him. Inside the fiery furnace built by man, the three youths lived because of a greater fire from the presence of God. They lived through man's fire because they loved God's fire—the fire of His holy presence. Immanuel arrived on the scene that day to the amazement of a watching world. It was the fire of God's presence that preserved their lives because God's purposes are to protect and preserve life, not to destroy it.

This is the fire of God's presence that does not kill us but cleanses and cures us. This is the good, right type of fire that God responds with when we worship, value and protect His holy presence. He is truly a wall of fire without and a fire within—God With Us and God Within Us. Let us fulfill our royal priestly duty and minister to Him with the praise and thanksgiving that is due His Holy Name. Let us dare to come close to Him, to tabernacle with Him... and live!

RESOURCES

Anderson, Neil T. & Towns, Elmer L., *Rivers of Revival*, Regal Books, Ventura, CA 1997

Ankerberg, John & Weldon, John, *The Secret Teachings of the Masonic Lodge*, Moody Press, Chicago, IL 1989

Baginski, Bodo J., *Reiki Universal Life Energy*, Life Rhythm Press, Mendocino, CA, 1988

Carlson, Ron & Decker, Ed, *Fast Facts on False Teachings*, Harvest House Publishers, Eugene, OR 1994

Dawson, Joy, *Intimate Friendship With God*, Chosen Books, Grand Rapids, MI 1986

DeHaan, M.R., M.D., *The Tabernacle*, Zondervan Publishing, Grand Rapids, MI, 1955

Frangipane, Francis, *The Power of One Christ-like Life*, Whitaker House, New Kensington, PA 1999

Grudem, Wayne, *Systematic Theology*, Zondervon Publishing House, Grand Rapids, MI 1994

Guiley, Rosemary Ellen, *Harpers Encyclopedia of Mystical & Paranormal Experiences*, Harper Collins, New York, N.Y. 1991

Hunt, Dave & McMahon, T.A., *The Seduction of Christianity,* Harvest House Publishers, Eugene, OR 1985

Horan, Paula, *Empowerment Through Reiki,* Lotus Light Publications, Wilmot, WI 1992

Jakes, T.D., *From The Cross To Pentecost,* Howard Books, New York, NY 2010

Joyner, Rick, *There Were Two Trees In The Garden,* Morningstar Publications, Charlotte, NC 1986

Karen, Michelle, *Astrology For Enlightenment,* Atria Books, New York, NY 2008

Morris, S. Brent, Ph.D., *The Idiots Guide to Freemasonry,* Alpha Publishing, New York, NY 2006

Olford, Stephen F., *The Tabernacle, Camping With God,* Kregel Publications, Grand Rapids, MI 1971

Rauser, Randal, *Finding God In The Shack,* Paternoster Publishing, Colorado Springs, CO 2009

Soltau, Henry W., *The Tabernacle, The Priesthood and The Offerings,* Kregel Publications, Grand Rapids, MI 1972

Stein, Diane, *Essential Reiki,* The Crossing Press, Freedom, CA 1995

Young, Wm. Paul, *The Shack,* Windblown Media, Newbury Park, CA 2007

Yungen, Ray, *For Many Shall Come In My Name,* Lighthouse Trails Publishing, Silverton, OR 2007

OTHER BOOKS
BY REFORM MINISTRY PUBLICATIONS

Available on Amazon
www.reformministry.com

Transforming The Queen, A Woman's Story of Personal Repentance

Take The Limits Off Of God!

Elijah Must Come First!

Seeing Behind The Mask, Spiritual Discernment For The Days Ahead

Recipe For Sharing

Confidence Shall Be Your Strength!

Made in United States
Troutdale, OR
02/21/2024

17875124R00086